THE ULTIMATE MATRIX SYST

The Ultimate physique of international bodybuilding champion Ian Riley.

THE ULTIMATE
MATRIX SYSTEM

Ronald S. Laura and
Kenneth R. Dutton

ALLEN & UNWIN

To my nephews, Jim Laura Jr, Chris Laura and the Rev. Jeffrey Collins—in appreciation of your willingness to become my first three Matrix trial subjects, all those years ago. Congratulations on staying with the Matrix system and for proving that it is possible to build a muscular and powerful body without the use of drugs. Wishing you the best always of health and fitness.

Ronald S. Laura

© R. S. Laura and K. R. Dutton, 1996

First published in 1996 by
Allen & Unwin Pty Ltd
9 Atchison Street, St Leonards, NSW 2065 Australia
Phone: (61 2) 9901 4088
Fax: (61 2) 9906 2218
E-mail: 100252.103@compuserve.com

National Library of Australia
Cataloguing-in-Publication entry:

Laura, R. S. (Ronald S.)
   The ultimate matrix system.

   ISBN 1 86373 8169.

   1. Weight training. I. Dutton, K. R. (Kenneth Raymond), 1938– . II. Title

613.713

Set in 10.5/12 Times by DOCUPRO, Sydney
Printed by South Wind Production Singapore Private Limited

10 9 8 7 6 5 4 3 2 1

The authors have great faith in this program but cannot take responsibility for injury caused to readers. As with any exercise program, it should be undertaken with care and with individuals working at their own pace. Seek your doctor's advice to ensure that you are in good health before embarking on this program.

Contents

Introduction

This is the final volume in the Matrix trilogy, the series of works that sets out and explains the Matrix system of weight training. The first volume in the series, *The Matrix Principle* (Allen & Unwin, Sydney, 1991), was directed at introducing the Matrix training method in the context of a holistic approach to exercise, fitness and health; it also set out the first twelve Matrix techniques (the Introductory techniques) and showed how they could form the basis of a one-year training regime. In its successor, *Matrix for Muscle Gain* (Allen & Unwin, Sydney, 1993), we concentrated on the physiology of muscle growth or hypertrophy, indicating how the Matrix patterns of full and partial repetitions worked to promote the hypertrophic response; this volume added a further twelve (Intermediate) Matrix techniques to those previously published, introducing them progressively into the training regime in order to provide an increasing level of challenge to the muscle system for those who had successfully completed the first year of Matrix training.

The overwhelming response of weight trainers to the first two volumes, and repeated requests from dedicated Matrix users for details of the pre-viously unpublished Advanced techniques, have led to the appearance of this third and final volume in the series. Other works by the present authors have dealt with particular applications of the Matrix system (*Weight Training for Sports*, Bantam, Sydney, 1993) or with simplified versions of it for non-specialists wishing to embark on an exercise regime (*Twelve Weeks to a Better Body for Women, Twelve Weeks to a Better Body for Men*, Allen & Unwin, Sydney, 1994). Planned future works include a guide to combin-ing Matrix and conventional weight training (the Matrix Combination System). However, the cornerstone of the system remains the total set of 36 Core Matrix techniques, of which twelve are introduced in each volume of the trilogy, the final twelve (Advanced) techniques being presented for the first time in the present work.

In addition to its part in the series, each Matrix volume incorporates a self-contained workout regime aimed at meeting the needs of trainers at various stages of development and/or of various degrees of experience with Matrix exercise. The latter group would include those dedicated Matrix trainers who have followed the two successive one-year programs in our earlier books and whose progress has led them to embark on a third year's training at a more advanced level. In addition to these long-standing 'converts' to Matrix training, however, the program provided here can be followed by elite weight trainers who have not used Matrix before, as well as by bodybuilders who are at, or approaching, competition standard.

For those who come to this book not having used the Matrix system before, it should be pointed out that the descriptions of Matrix movement patterns are given in summary form only, in order not to repeat material included in earlier volumes. For this reason, such readers would be advised to consult one of the earlier books, in which the movement patterns are described in greater detail. Equally, descriptions of the exercises are not given, as trainers are expected to be already familiar with them. Most of the exercises, however, are illustrated in the photographs.

Fundamentally though, this book is not written for newcomers, but for committed Matrix trainers, in response to both their needs and their requests. Most of them do not see themselves as competitors or even potential competitors in bodybuilding competition—in many cases because a contest appearance has little appeal to them rather than because of the lack of quality of their physique. What they are mainly interested in is improved strength, the development of advanced and harmonious muscularity, and an increase in overall fitness. Above all, they are seeking to achieve these goals without recourse to anabolic steroids, growth hormone, or any of the other harmful and often illicit substances which have bedevilled the world of bodybuilding and often brought it into ill repute.

It cannot be stated too strongly that our major motivation in developing and making known the Matrix system was to present a method of weight training which had been found so effective that those who stuck to it rigorously would be able to achieve, by natural means, results equivalent to those normally associated with steroid use. It was our hope that the effectiveness of the program would attract many trainers who did not feel drawn to the drug culture, but had been tempted to resort to steroids simply because their conventional training was not achieving the results they sought. It is gratifying to know that some thousands of trainers world-wide have adopted the Matrix system as a natural alternative to growth-producing drugs; many of them have testified to its effectiveness in this regard either by personal accounts or in correspondence held by the authors.

It must immediately be acknowledged that we are aware of a number of trainers who use Matrix techniques and at the same time, particularly if they are competitive bodybuilders, also use anabolic steroids. That, of course, is their choice (and, usually, a choice made in full knowledge of the legal, ethical and physical consequences of their decision). There is, needless to say, no way that we can, or would wish to, restrict Matrix exercise to drug-free trainers. All that we can do in this regard is, first, to draw attention to the chapter on ergogenic drugs in our earlier book *The Matrix Principle* (pp. 78–84) and in particular to the potentially lethal effects of anabolic steroids; and, second, to reiterate the philosophy underlying our whole approach to weight training—namely, that we see it as part of a total 'matrix' of lifestyle-related factors, including the avoidance of harmful substances, moderation in eating and drinking habits, and other practices aimed at promoting fitness, health and overall well-being. Although an anabolic steroid user may engage in Matrix weight training, this is not the same thing as following the Matrix system—a total system including exercise, diet and lifestyle, which involves a holistic approach to the way we treat our bodies.

More will be said about this approach in chapter 4, which takes up and expands some of the points made in *The Matrix Principle*. As the introductory volume in the series, *The Matrix Principle* was able to touch only relatively briefly on a number of the factors on which the Matrix system is built, and we have therefore taken the opportunity in succeeding volumes to expand on some of the more important of these. In *Matrix for Muscle Gain*, we focused chiefly upon the physiology of the muscle system and the mechanisms by which particular patterns or types of muscular contraction are more likely than others to elicit the hypertrophic or muscle-building response. In the present volume, we pass to another aspect of weight exercise to which only fairly brief attention could be paid in earlier books—namely the role of neuromuscular processes, the 'mind-to-muscle signals' on which we rely for any form of voluntary muscular activity.

In the five years or so following the appearance of *The Matrix Principle*, a number of contributions to the serious literature on weight training and physical exercise have brought confirmation to both the general approach and some of the individual arguments advanced in the earlier work. This is not to say that the Matrix system has been without its critics, and the opportunity will be taken here to indicate some of the queries and criticisms raised and to respond to them. On the whole, however, the authors have been encouraged by the increasing acceptance of their approach to weight training on the part of trainers and theorists alike, as well as a growing interest in scientific circles—especially in the neurosciences—relating to the potentialities of the neuromuscular system which the Matrix approach seeks to exploit more fully than other systems. In the chapters that follow, some of the recent findings in this area will be described and their practical relevance for the weight trainer explored.

Professor Ronald Laura as he appeared in an advertisement for the Cenatuar computer.

Part 1

Matrix, muscles and the mind

The Matrix-built physique of 18-year-old Adam Laura.

1 A new look at Matrix training

Any new system of weight training, like any new product coming on to the market, needs to be thoroughly evaluated if it is to achieve credibility in the long term. This is even more obviously the case when a system is claimed to represent a 'revolution' or 'breakthrough' as compared with longer-established, traditional or more orthodox systems. Such claims are made with almost monotonous regularity in the world of weight training, where uncritical acceptance of the latest fad can often be counted on from trainers desperate to try anything in their quest for the elusive goal of highly developed muscularity.

In this general climate, it may be appropriate to take the opportunity afforded by the presentation of the final Matrix techniques to recapitulate the salient points of the Matrix training system, and to attempt to place them in perspective so that an accurate evaluation can be attempted. The feedback received from readers and trainers in the years since the publication of the first volume in the series has been helpful in identifying a number of misconceptions and areas requiring further explanation, while much of the weight-training literature that has appeared over the same period has brought a new relevance to issues raised in our previous works. Both these factors have suggested that some kind of overview of the Matrix approach may now be timely.

Background

The Matrix weight-training system was devised by Professor R. S. Laura, a former world champion powerlifter and international (IFBB) bodybuilding judge with extensive experience in the training of weightlifters and bodybuilders. Both in his own personal training and in the preparation of elite bodybuilders for world-class competition, Professor Laura had for some years been experimenting with various methods of incorporating part-repetitions and high-intensity repetition patterns into the training regime, with a view to improving its effectiveness and to achieving potentially superior results to those derived from conventional ten-repetition sets with increasingly heavier weights. Some of these early forerunners of Matrix training are described in our earlier works.

At the same time, as an academic with qualifications in philosophy and bioethics, Professor Laura had been engaged in research on the history and development of biomedical concepts and their application to human health, a subject on which he had authored a number of papers in scholarly journals. In particular, this research had to do with the extent to which the diagnosis and treatment of patients had become fragmented over the course of the eighteenth to twentieth centuries, the result of a 'reductionist' approach to medical knowledge (and scientific knowledge in general) which concentrated on isolated symptoms and drew attention away from the treatment of the whole person or the human organism in its entirety. In much the same way, it could be seen that our concepts of exercise and even fitness had been allowed to develop as if they were somehow independent entities and could be isolated from the much broader issue of human health and well-being.

The most obvious case in point related to anabolic steroid use. In this case, an activity (bodybuilding) supposedly engaged in to promote physical fitness and health was transformed into precisely its opposite, owing to the detrimental and potentially life-threatening effects of steroid use. Other examples—smoking, obsessive/compulsive eating disorders such as anorexia and bulimia, and the like—served to underline the fact that many exercisers, including (even especially!) those prepared to spend large amounts of time and energy on their training, were in fact working towards two opposing goals: ostensibly attempting to build fitter bodies through exercise, while at the same time jeopardising this fitness through practices which were the very opposite of healthy.

It was out of considerations such as these that the Matrix system was born. From the consciousness that the health of the total human system was a product of a number of factors, all of them interactive, was born the notion of using the model of an interactive system (commonly known in the biological sciences and the world of computers as a 'matrix') as the basis of a holistic approach to health promotion in which exercise would play a vital part.

At the same time as the general Matrix system was being developed, experimentation with light-weight intensive exercise had begun to reveal encouraging results. The decision was therefore made to conduct a series of controlled tests in which groups of trainers using conventional weight training methods (sets of ten at greater than 70% of maximum single rep strength) were compared with similar groups—matched for all relevant criteria (age, training experience, workout frequency, diet, etc.)—using part-repetitions of lighter weights in various patterns, which were later to be codified as the Introductory Matrix patterns. In view of the relevance of these tests to the sport of bodybuilding, the research arm of the IFBB—the

Adam Parer demonstrates the kind of physique that can be built without the use of drugs.

official body representing bodybuilding at the international sporting level—asked its Australian branch (the Human Performance Research Centre) to undertake a series of developmental tests of the Matrix training method under Professor Laura's supervision. In the course of these tests, hundreds of patterns of movement were devised and were trialled by individual groups; of these patterns, 36 were eventually selected on the basis both of user response and of perceived effectiveness in muscle fibre recruitment, and it is these patterns, graded according to degree of difficulty, that make up the complete Matrix training system.

In addition to the trials conducted by the Human Performance Research Centre in Australia, further controlled tests of Matrix exercise patterns were carried out at the Harvard University Fitness Center. In both cases, the matched groups of participants maintained training diaries, which enabled direct comparisons to be made between Matrix trainers and conventional trainers who had been exposed to similar training experience, frequency of training, and dietary regimes. Equally, control and Matrix groups were carefully cross-matched for age, commencing fitness level and other relevant factors. The results of these trials were reported in the earlier work *The Matrix Principle*, notably the finding of substantially greater strength and size gains overall in the Matrix group as compared with the conventional control group.

The *overall* nature of these findings needs to be stressed: it is not claimed—nor has it ever been claimed by the authors—that every Matrix trainer made more substantial gains than every conventional trainer, or even (allowing for trainers of similar age, fitness and experience) that in every case the Matrix trainer showed superior results to the most closely matched conventional trainer. What the trial results indicated was that, despite individual variations and fluctuations, *on average* the Matrix trainers made greater gains in strength and muscle size (as determined by set measurements applied to all trainers) than was the case with conventional weight trainers. In some, although not all, individual cases, Matrix trainers made strength gains twice those of the most closely matched members of the conventional group, and muscle size gains three times as great.

Training theories and myths

On the basis of these trials, the decision was made to incorporate the first twelve Matrix techniques in a book setting out a one-year Introductory course. The twelve techniques selected as Introductory were those which, at the time of publication, had been tested over several years by successive groups of 'beginners' (i.e. newcomers to Matrix training) and found to be the most easily learnt and readily mastered. (More challenging techniques, with the benefit of further testing since the appearance of the first volume, have been incorporated into the Intermediate and Advanced courses.)

The initial book in the series, *The Matrix Principle*, thus had a twofold aim :

- first, to introduce trainers to the concept of Matrix training;
- and second, to set the Matrix training regime in the context of a holistic approach to health and fitness.

The question next confronting the authors was how this aim might best be pursued, given the novelty of the Matrix training method and its challenge to many traditional weight-training assumptions. In particular, it could be anticipated that such an innovative approach to training would meet with resistance from those with a vested interest in conventional training methods, and even more so from within the ranks of professional 'sports scientists', some of whom could be expected to resent the entry of outsiders into their closely guarded professional domain.

The authors took the conscious decision to meet these issues head on. As professional educators, they were struck by what might be called the 'mythology' of weight training—the uncritically accepted assumptions and long-held dogmas which affected the popular literature of bodybuilding and even found their way into the mind-set of some professional physical educators and academic sports scientists. It seemed appropriate, then, to use the opportunity of a new approach and innovative style of exercise in order to challenge some of the deeply ingrained but often unjustifiable attitudes pervading the world of weight training.

In the first instance, it was impossible not to be aware of the substantial gap separating, on the one hand, the serious academic area of exercise physiology—a branch of human physiology, in which recent advances in knowledge were recorded in specialist journal articles and conference papers—and, on the other, the world of bodybuilding 'folklore' with its ancient myths and untested personal prejudices. To bridge this gap, we felt, would be in itself a useful achievement, given that the vast majority of trainers were not conversant with the serious literature or able to follow much of its technicalities of language and concept. Not that the authors purported to be exercise physiologists, biomechanicists or professional scientists; on the contrary, we have been careful to indicate in our writings that, while we have extensive practical experience as trainers and instructors, our professional expertise lies in the *educational* process, and in the methodologies whereby teaching and learning are most effectively carried out. As academics, however, who were able to read and follow the scientific literature (even if not contributing professionally to it), we were uniquely well placed to use this access to the latest theoretical knowledge as the basis of practical programs geared to the needs of actual trainers. Our task, in this regard, was the educator's task rather than that of the investigative scientist or original researcher, and it is important that this distinction be clearly recognised. We are extremely grateful for the support and encouragement we have received from scientific colleagues, working in areas relevant to exercise and training, who have acknowledged our interest in their work and our desire to follow up its practical application in concrete programs, but we do not confuse our own pedagogical role with their scientific role. As educators, our aim has been to put ourselves into the shoes of weight trainers and to provide them with information existing in the public domain but needing to be translated into more readily accessible form. This, indeed, is the primary task of the educator.

The second area in which the Matrix approach has challenged preconceived notions relates to the demonstrated effectiveness of Matrix training. To a number of gym instructors and trainers, the Matrix system could not possibly work, for the simple reason that it used lighter than conventional weights. When asked for the basis of this conclusion, such trainers typically responded by saying that it was 'a well known fact' that only heavy weights were conducive to muscle growth; light weights, it was equally 'well known', were suitable only for shaping some body parts and improving definition. This is, of course, the conventional wisdom of weight training, and is strongly held not only by many of the older generation of trainers but even by many of their pupils among the younger generation. It should be made clear that we have never set out to deny categorically the conventional view: a careful reading of *The Matrix Principle* will indicate that we saw the simplistic division of light and heavy work as 'unnecessarily limiting' (p. 24), but to interpret the Matrix system as somehow an attack on heavy weights is to misconstrue it completely. Indeed, as mentioned in the introduction, a forthcoming work will set out a number of routines in which Matrix and conventional (i.e. moderate to heavy) weight workouts are combined.

More particularly, it would be totally incorrect to interpret the Matrix approach as an 'attack on' anything—except perhaps ignorance, bigotry and hypocrisy in the world of weight training. Our aim has never been to attack anyone else's training methods, since almost every method has something to be said in its favour, but merely to indicate that it was worth looking beyond the conventional light weight/heavy weight divide, and asking whether lighter weights used in innovative ways might not prove highly effective. Not having set out to attack or condemn any other weight training system, we are not in the least defensive and are entirely open to intelligent criticism wherever it is put forward.

How, then, were the authors to set about dealing with the light weight/heavy weight divide? A fully scientific approach would require testing the lighter-weight system and comparing the results with the conventional system—and this, as stated above, is precisely the approach that the authors took. The point would not be worth labouring, but for the fact that some have responded to the Matrix approach simply by the statement: 'It can't work'. Such a response must surely be as unscientific—indeed, as anti-scientific—as can be imagined. The properly scientific response to a new concept or theory is not to deny it outright, but to question on what evidence it is based.

If the evidence is that a system works despite preconceived theory, then it is the theory that needs re-thinking rather than the system that needs re-designing. But it is instructive to ask, in this case, what is the basis of the preconceived theory itself (i.e. that only heavy-weight work leads to muscle growth)? The answer, of necessity, must be that at some stage or other heavy-weight work was observed to lead to muscle growth—in other words, exactly the same test as was applied to Matrix exercise in the controlled trials.

The plain fact of the matter is that we are here in a world where scientific knowledge is still in an imperfect state. The point was made in our second volume (*Matrix for Muscle Gain*) that the exact causes of muscle hypertrophy are still not known with absolute certainty—although much is known, and increasingly so, about the kinds of exercise factors likely to lead to a hypertrophic response. Indeed, much of the discussion in the second book was devoted to indicating how Matrix exercise belonged to categories of muscle movement which had been associated with hypertrophy. The point is that, given the present state of knowledge, it is not scientifically possible to claim categorically that a form of exercise cannot work: as in the case of conventional weight exercise, so in the case of Matrix training, all that can be validly done is to look at its *results*, and if necessary refine the theory so that it accords with the results rather than the other way around.

The Matrix approach

That the above discussion should even be necessary is itself an interesting commentary on the world of weight training, characterised as it often is by a blind adherence to unscientific theory and by an unquestioning belief in supposed authority. Regrettably, such attitudes are often fostered by popular articles with headings such as 'Training Secrets of the Champions', 'The Secret Formula for Success', and the like. The impression is fostered that there is some mystical or magical 'knowledge', to which certain trainers or product promoters have access, and into which less experienced trainers can be initiated—sometimes for a substantial fee, but more usually by reading the article in question and blindly following the weight regime it sets out. Again, we are not criticising the product promoters or the authors of the training articles—frequently, the latter are helpful and effective. What we *are* critical of is the mentality or approach which suggests that there is some mystical bodybuilding 'lore', some secrets of success which are known only to the experts and their pupils.

In fact, of course, there is no such thing. There is only human physiology, nothing more or less than that. Human physiology works according to certain principles—many of which have been discovered, although many are still the subject of ongoing research—but it is a *science* and not a mystery religion. Our point may perhaps best be clarified by recounting a situation which the authors encounter with amazing frequency. Our works on weight training having given us a reputation as 'authorities', we are approached by a particularly keen young trainer, anxious to get the most out of his (for it is usually a male) workout regime. His question, typically, will be along the lines of: 'How many reps of such-and-such an exercise should I do?' We can be almost 100 per cent certain—and, indeed, we have tested this hypothesis from time to time—that if we were to reply, in a tone of great authority: 'You should *never* do a set of more than seven reps', or, alternatively: 'Sets of anything less than 25 reps are practically useless', the trainer will thank us for the advice and will later be seen in some corner of the gym slavishly carrying it out. Remarkably, the young trainers we are talking about are university students. More amazingly still, more than a few of them are science students!

This attitude is so widely prevalent in the world of weight training that the above situation will be recognised by most senior instructors, and certainly those to whom we have mentioned it have confirmed how closely it has paralleled their own experience. The fault, perhaps, lies not so much with the keen young trainers themselves as with those who have conditioned them into the belief that there is a kind of superior knowledge possessed by training 'gurus', with the result that authoritative statements, even if in all appearance contrary to common sense, are accepted without question.

It was our conviction of the need to overcome this attitude that led us to approach the training issue in a way we believed to be basically more honest and true to the facts, as well as making more sense from the pedagogical point of view. In *The Matrix Principle*, we began with a typical trainer's question: 'What do I do to build up my shoulders?', and showed how—rather than simply providing a dogmatic answer ('Do three sets of ten lateral raises with 20 lb dumbbells twice a week')—one might set about instructing the trainer in how muscles, including the shoulder muscles, work. Work, that is, mechanically, physiologically, chemically, and in the neuro-transmission function. As a result of this teaching process—much longer, admittedly, than the simple dogmatic answer, but ultimately much more satisfying—the beginning trainer would be able to *answer his or her own question*. This, we pointed out, was the aim of all serious learning—to become self-directed, free of reliance on the agency of the teacher and being subject only to the facts as they could be ascertained directly by the learner.

In the same vein, we have tried to avoid too narrowly prescriptive an approach to the performance of Matrix exercise; it is important to understand that the Matrix routines provided here and in our other books are to be taken as a guide only. The point cannot be too strongly stressed that we are presenting a weight-training *principle*, a method of using a variety of repetition patterns to enhance the muscle fibre recruitment process. In this sense, as we have made clear in earlier volumes, trainers can themselves use the Matrix Principle to devise their own patterns of repetition, or can invent variations on any of the 36 techniques included in the standard Matrix system. The techniques listed by us are not intended as a prescriptive list to be adhered to slavishly: rather, they are to be taken as representing the fruits of exhaustive testing of potential techniques with a large number of trainers over several years and, as such, are put forward as a helpful guide to what has been found to work well, rather than as a set of commands to be obeyed to the letter. Similarly, the routines for each body part are meant to save trainers the trouble of working out their own Matrix routine based on the standard body part exercises. But, once again, trainers—especially advanced trainers—may well have an alternative routine which seems to suit their training style, and there is no reason why such a routine, or selected parts of it, should not be carried out in Matrix mode.

Assuming that most trainers who use this book will already have worked their way through the routines given in earlier volumes, the above point will need no elaboration as it will be consistent with one of the two most common exercise strategies adopted by dedicated Matrix trainers. Some prefer to stick quite rigorously to the programs as given—not out of the blind adherence we condemned above, but simply because they are happy to stay with routines that have been tested and shown to be effective. Other trainers, however, prefer to take a more creative approach, usually by way of variations in the particular exercises or the particular techniques specified for individual exercises, depending on their own perception of how their body best responds to individual exercises and/or techniques. Both kinds of trainer, however, will be familiar with the 'style' of Matrix exercise and for that reason will have no difficulty with the repetition patterns. For those who have come to this book without previous experience of the Matrix system, however, a word about the movement patterns might perhaps be warranted at this point.

One of the least comprehending criticisms levelled at the Matrix system on its first appearance was that it consisted of such a complex arrangement of movements, part-movements, pauses and the like, that trainers would either need to be constantly referring to the manual or would need to be equipped with an abacus and stopwatch if they were ever to follow its complications. Such comments were invariably made by reviewers who had manifestly not tried Matrix exercise for themselves, and occasionally by newer trainers who had not yet become accustomed to the repetition patterns and who assumed they never would. In fact, as all those who have persevered for a few weeks will attest, the Matrix patterns are indeed *patterns*: each works according to one or more simple principles (symmetry; ascending order; descending order, etc.) which are quickly mastered and thereafter hardly require a conscious effort of the memory, any more than does, say, learning to play a new piece of music on a musical instrument. In both cases there is an initial effort of committing something to memory, but thereafter the 'pattern' becomes ingrained in both the consciousness and, as it were, the body's own 'memory'.

The mind in bodybuilding

The role of mental processes in the training experience is one of the most topical issues in contemporary weight-training theory. To open almost any bodybuilding or fitness magazine published in the last couple of years is to find at least one article, if not several, devoted to the role of mental processes in the exercise or fitness regime. In some of these publications, there is now a regular department given over to the subject, which is obviously seen as a 'hot' topic about which readers are anxious to be informed. The content of these articles varies considerably in nature and quality, from the substantial to the superficial and from the practical and useful to the vague and fanciful. Two themes predominate, both of them potentially of value to the serious trainer: first, the relationship of exercise to mental stress, its role in reducing tension and fostering a sense of relaxation and well-being; and second, the potential of bodybuilding and weight training for bolstering self-confidence and improving motivation. These articles, or at least the best of them, fulfil a useful role in translating into the world of weight exercise some of the more important insights from the area of sports psychology—a growing field which has proved its effectiveness in a number of athletic and team sports and whose relevance to bodybuilding and weight training was too long ignored.

Among these articles, although rather more rarely, the reader will come across a reference to the involvement of mental processes in the weight

Weight training should engage the mind as well as the body.

workout itself. In view of the increasing interest in what is commonly known as the 'mind–body connection', there is surprisingly little concentration on how this connection can be used to increase the effectiveness of the actual workout. The few articles devoted to the topic in the bodybuilding and fitness literature tend to raise interesting possibilities, but in general do little more than scratch the surface of this admittedly complex subject. Our aim here is to explore some of the more recent thinking in the area of the neurosciences (psychology and neurophysiology), with a view to showing just how relevant contemporary scientific research may be to something as apparently distant and unrelated as the gym workout.

Our method of proceeding will be to move from the practical training situation to increasingly more theoretical issues. The reason for this is twofold: first, those whose interest in the subject is restricted to its practical implications for their day-to-day training may not wish to read this section in its entirety but may 'switch off' once the discussion moves further into the area of theory; and second, by beginning with practice and moving to theory (and reversing the usual pedagogical order) we hope to bring out the relevance of the quoted scientific studies to the practical situation—a relationship which might be more difficult to grasp were we to begin at the scientific 'end' of the discussion.

For the moment, however, it may be apposite to point out that the main issues that we have discussed in the preceding pages all relate, in one way or another, to the role of the mind. At this point, let us briefly draw attention to the theme underlying the points we have made, and its relationship to mental involvement in the training process. In summary :

- the Matrix system is a holistic approach to fitness and health, involving mental attitudes as much as physical activity. In particular, it is meant to combat those forms of mental aberration which lead people to resort to drugs in order to feed their obsessions;
- Matrix weight training is based on the results of controlled tests comparing Matrix and conventional training. The claims made for it are not dogmatic statements, but observations made on the results of the trials. This we believe to be an intellectually defensible approach, and the only basis on which a weight-training system can logically be evaluated;
- our presentation of Matrix training has deliberately avoided the prescriptive, dogmatic mode in favour of our appeal to the trainer's reason and commonsense. We believe that weight trainers are capable of using their own intellect to follow a non-technical but accurate account of muscle function and development, the aim of which is to provide trainers with the information that will allow them to answer their own questions.

In the chapters that follow, we shall explore in greater detail the ways in which our mental processes contribute to muscular activity, and shall examine ways of using our mental perceptions to add to the effectiveness of the weight workout.

2 Weights and repetitions

To begin our analysis by considering the practical training situation, we can take as our starting point the perennial question of how heavy the training weight should be. Although some training manuals and articles actually prescribe given weights for individual exercises, a moment's reflection will remind us of the obvious fact that appropriate training weights will vary from one trainer to another, depending on age, sex, size, strength, training history and the like. The traditional way of converting these individual differences to a common scale is to express the training weight as a percentage of a 'single-rep maximum'—that is, the maximum weight that the particular trainer can lift for that movement in a single repetition performed strictly. The conventional definition of 'heavy-weight' training is training done with weights of 70% or more of a single-rep maximum; 'moderate-weight' training is usually defined as between 50% and 70%; and 'light-weight' training as less than 50% of a single-rep maximum. The question of training poundages can thus be posed as: what percentage of my single-rep maximum should I use? The question is no doubt as old as weight training itself, and certainly any perusal of training manuals and magazines of the last 50 years or so will confirm its status as the prime recurring training question.

Suppose, then, that we wish to discover the most up-to-date thinking on this issue, and turn to recent articles in the most respected bodybuilding magazines. Surprisingly, perhaps, we shall find that the debate is still far from settled. Here are two extracts from recent articles by highly qualified weight training writers:

> The only factor that dictates muscle-fiber activation is how *heavy* the weight is . . . The heavier the weight, the more fibers are recruited to lift it, meaning that more fibers will be stimulated to grow larger (hypertrophy). It's heavy weights . . . and high muscular output over a given unit of time that stimulates maximum muscle growth—and nothing else.[1]

> Many bodybuilding programs today encourage the use of maximum poundages for low repetitions . . . to achieve muscle growth. The

14

proponents of this type of training argue that heavy lifting is needed to stimulate the maximum number of muscle fibers. However, I have presented evidence . . . that supports the view that heavy training *does not* stimulate significantly more muscle fibers than a program that emphasises moderate poundages (less than 70% of a single repetition maximum).[2]

The reader of these two articles (by John Little and Douglas Crist respectively) might be forgiven for concluding that not only does the age-old controversy show no sign of abating, but also that the question of light, moderate or heavy weights is as much a matter of conjecture and conflicting hypotheses as it ever was. In the light of this situation, it is hardly surprising that many trainers find the question of weight the most confused, and confusing, issue in the whole area of weight training.

Light or heavy?

One of the main purposes of this chapter is to attempt to shed a little light on the heaviness question by examining some of the basic premises on which protagonists on either side of the question establish their theories. Readers will be well aware that Matrix training is based on the use of light-to-moderate weights (40% of a single-rep maximum is usually suggested for beginners, although more advanced trainers will progress well into the upper levels of the moderate range), so our position in this debate could be assumed to be predictably on the one side rather than on the other. To some extent this is true, but only in the sense that we distance ourselves from the view that heavy-weight training is the *only* means of attaining significant muscle growth. We do believe, on the other hand, that heavy-weight training can be remarkably effective, as most professional bodybuilders will testify. In short, our position is that certain forms of moderate, and even light, resistance exercise can achieve hypertrophic effects similar to those of heavy training but without the attendant problems and risks of heavy weights.

To return, then, to the divergent views put forward by John Little and Douglas Crist, it is important to recognise that the very different conclusions at which they arrive are due, at least in part, to differences in their initial premise. To understand this, we may trace the lines of their arguments and see where they lead.

John Little's article is by way of a critique of 'multiple-angle training'—that is, the belief that by hitting the muscle from a variety of different angles, you will stimulate more muscle fibres. To this simplistic view, Little justifiably responds that by limiting the stress of focus to one region of a muscle group—the aim of multiple-angle training—the trainer actually *reduces* the potential fibre involvement of that exercise. In any case, he points out, multiple-angle training may not isolate part of a muscle, since the whole muscle complex is often called into action simultaneously. His conclusion is well worth quoting:

It doesn't matter to the body whether you train with an incline bench, a decline bench or a flat bench. For that matter, your muscles can't differentiate between barbells, a Nautilus machine or a suitcase filled with rocks. All your muscles are concerned with is whether enough fibers have been recruited to get the job done (i.e. move the resistance).[3]

In this context, Little's preference for relatively heavy weight makes obvious sense: that is, in the context of whole muscle-group exercise as distinct from isolation-type work.

We shall return to the question of isolation a little later. First, let us consider the arguments that lead Douglas M. Crist to reject the notion of heavy training in favour of moderate weights and high repetitions. He points out that there are two processes involved in muscular exercise: first, the transport of substances from the nerve cells to terminal points connected to muscle fibres; and second, the influence of those substances on muscle function and growth. The aim of the training program should therefore be to stimulate the muscle to the maximum (the second process) while not straining nerve-discharge reserves (the first process). If the latter occurs, the result is the 'overtraining' syndrome. Crist's conclusion is that 'the key to bodybuilding success has less to do with muscle fibers than the nerves that regulate the muscle fiber response characteristics'.[4] He provides a telling illustration of just how crucial is the input of the nervous system (a process known as *neurotropism*) into the control of muscle fibre function:

A nerve that connects to a slow-twitch, endurance muscle fiber is smaller in diameter than a nerve that connects to a more powerful fast-twitch muscle fiber. However, if these nerves are disconnected from their original muscle fibers and then crossed over to the other fibers, the muscle fibers will undergo dramatic changes (*Nature* 257:602, 1975; 206:831, 1965). The slow-twitch endurance fiber will take on the characteristics of the more powerful fast-twitch fiber, while the fast-twitch fiber will take on the characteristics of the endurance fiber.[5]

In other words, either of the two broad types of muscle fibre[6] will take on the characteristics of the other once the source of the nerve supply is reversed. The significance of this finding is considerable, as it indicates the vital role of the nervous system in determining muscular response.

What Little and Crist both acknowledge in their articles, despite starting from very different premises and reaching very different conclusions, is the importance of the 'signalling system' which orders the muscles to perform their work—and, indirectly, the extent to which this system can be manipulated, or even, as it were, 'tricked' by forces applied to it either voluntarily or involuntarily. John Little points out that the muscles do not 'know' what force is being applied to them: as we pointed out in *The Matrix Principle*, the muscles 'know' only an electronic stimulus which is mediated to them with greater or lesser force. Similarly, Douglas Crist draws attention to the power of the stimulus mechanism in determining muscle behaviour (including metabolism, growth and function). Both writers, each approaching the

Note how the configuration of the back muscles alters during the Lat Pulldown.

subject from a different point of view, are led to recognise that the crucial factor in muscle fibre recruitment is the *message received* by the muscle fibres, that they are the recipients rather than the initiators of decisions as to how much fibre activation needs to take place.

It may be objected that John Little's view appears, at least superficially, to accord total primacy to the actual load over the signalling process—that is, his advocacy of heavy weight leaves little room for Crist's distinction between the 'upstream' and 'downstream' activity relative to the myoneural junction (the connection of nerve and muscle fibre). In other articles, however, John Little has pointed out that 'if adequate *stimulation* is present, muscle will grow—period. And it will grow quickly in proportion to the severity of the stimulation.'[7] This stimulation, Little argues, is maximal when exercise is intense, intensity value being determined by amount of overload (how heavy the weights are) and rate of work (amount lifted per minute). Following through with this approach, Little argues that full repetitions simply do not allow maximum overload because there is always a weaker part of the range (e.g. the first few centimetres of the bench press). His solution to this problem is to train only in the strongest part of the range, using the heaviest possible weights. Underlying Little's conclusion is the fact that the muscles do not 'know' whether they are working in the full range or not—all that matters is that they receive the message to recruit the maximum number of fibres.

The point being made here is that, even in two such widely divergent views of the most effective way to build muscle, there is a certain amount of common ground. Both writers agree that to obtain maximal muscle fibre stimulation is not purely a matter of lifting a heavy weight: Crist's advocacy of high repetitions and high numbers of sets, and Little's recognition of the *rate* of work (i.e. not just pounds lifted, but pounds per unit of time) are, for all their differences, a recognition of *intensity* as the key (or a crucial element of it) to muscle fibre stimulation.

The question, then, arises how far the intensity of muscle fibre stimulation is dependent on the heaviness of the load and how far it is dependent on repetition (or *rate* of work). That a number of repetitions performed in immediate succession is a vital element of intensity is well attested— otherwise a single rep of each exercise, performed at maximum weight, would suffice—and workouts would be a lot shorter! But with regard to the actual weight which is repeatedly moved, it is not so obvious that a heavy weight is required for optimum results. To use John Little's metaphor once again, the muscle does not 'know' how heavy the weight is. To use a crude analogy, let us say that a particular exercise involves lifting 600 lb over the course of a set. Most writers will readily agree that a single rep of 600 lb (if we could manage it) would not be optimally effective, and everyone will agree that 600 reps of a 1 lb weight would likewise be ineffective; but between 6 reps of 100 lb, and 10 reps of 60 lb, opinions will no doubt differ.

Even the most ardent advocates of light-to-moderate training will agree that the weight needs to be heavy enough to provide a certain amount of resistance to the muscles. What in fact happens is that, in a process known as proprioception, the muscle meets with resistance and feeds this informa- tion to the central nervous system, which in return provides a degree of stimulation to the muscle fibres proportionate to the resistance offered by the weight: this stimulation results in a shortening of the muscle and consequent movement of the limb.

We thus have a two-way process of transmission: muscle to nervous system, nervous system to muscle. The point of light-to-moderate weight training is that the particular element of muscle fibre stimulation which derives from repetition is not in a linear relationship to the heaviness of the weight, but increases progressively till it reaches a peak, after which tiredness begins to inhibit fibre recruitment. The weight, and its resistance, remain constant: the nerve-to-muscle signal changes from one rep to another, however, as more and more muscle fibres are recruited. The advocates of moderate-weight training would say that this type of training permits maximum fibre recruitment to be achieved (over a large number of reps) before tiredness takes over, whereas heavy-weight training causes muscle tiredness to occur too early and too intrusively. In Crist's words:

Lifting moderate poundages for a relatively high number of sets and repetitions recruits most—if not all—available muscle fibers. This type of weight training also stimulates neurotropic pathways to the muscle fibers, while at the same time it avoids high discharge rates and associated nervous system exhaustion.[8]

On the other hand, the proponents of heavy-weight training tend to place more reliance on force requirements (the muscle-to-mind message) than on motor neuron stimulation (the mind-to-muscle message), leaving it to the sheer energy output involved in shifting the load to provide the fibre recruitment required for growth. As John Little puts it:

With strongest range training, the heavier weight employed necessitates greater energy production in terms of what's necessary to fuel increased fiber recruitment and muscular output. As clinical studies have empirically demonstrated time and again, this is the only stimulus that induces muscle growth.[9]

The energy output involved in heavy-weight training is such that re-cuperation times tend to be longer than with moderate-to-light training; in the latter case, the muscular recovery needs tend to be mainly local, whereas in the former they tend to affect the system as a whole.

Effective training method

Where has this discussion of the perennial weight-level controversy led us? Our own conclusion is that it has revealed the argument to be somewhat misplaced—at least, to the extent to which we are asked to believe that one training method, and one alone, will lead to maximum muscle growth. The process of muscle activation, we have seen, is a complex one, involving a 'loop' of information from muscle to nervous system and back again. Messages can be initiated at various points in the loop, and the training method we use will largely determine which point has priority—the point of initial force, or the myoneural junction at which the muscle is ordered to contract. Confirmation of this view has come from two scientific exper-iments. The first was carried out on mice exposed to weightlessness during US space exploration programs. This pointed to the role of initial resistance in indicating to the body's control mechanisms that a forceful muscular response is required: studies of mouse soleus muscle indicated that, under weightless conditions, many of the muscle fibres had actually changed from fast-twitch (strength) muscle to slow-twitch (endurance) muscle.[10] On the other hand, this finding should be placed alongside the data from the second experiment—namely, research reported by Douglas Crist (above), whereby precisely the same fibre-type change resulted from switching nervous inputs into the muscle. It is clear, then, that the 'message loop' can be activated at one point or the other. It is, to a large extent, a matter of emphasis or degree whether our training stresses one or the other point of the information loop.

Just as importantly, however, our discussion has opened up some interesting possibilities. In the next chapter, we shall explore in greater detail the crucial role of the nerve-to-muscle signalling system, with a view to suggesting how its part in the muscle-activating process can be maximised. For the moment, our concern has been to indicate that this is only part of the total process of muscle activation, and that there is still an important role for the resistance provided by moderate-to-heavy weight in muscle building.

Before leaving this issue, however, there is an aspect of the training-weight controversy on which it will be helpful at this stage to spend a little more time. John Little's heavy-weight training method, it will be recalled, was based on two postulates:

1. that by hitting the whole muscle group with a heavy weight, you are maximising the potential number of muscle fibres involved; this method he contrasts with multiple-angle training and other methods based on isolation which limit the focus of the stress on the muscle group;
2. that part-repetitions in the strongest part of the range enable the muscle to be hit just as fully as by full-range reps—the difference being that the part-reps enable a heavier weight to be used since they eliminate the weak part of the muscle's range of movement (that part of the range for which the weight will be too heavy).

There is no doubt that this training method can be extremely effective, notably in training for strength and explosive power. It is not uncommon, for instance, for top sprinters to do leg presses of 1000 lb or more—even one-leg presses with this weight—in the first quarter or so of the total range, to build up the power required to shift the body at maximum speed.[11]

Once again, however, we must return to our point that the fact that a training method can be effective does not necessarily mean that it is the *only* method that is effective. Let us turn to the implications of the heavy-weight training method described above: whole muscle-group (as distinct from isolation) and strongest-range (as distinct from total range) part-repetitions. These two aspects are in fact intertwined, and can be dealt with together.

Broadly speaking, we can divide the standard repertoire of weight-training exercises into two kinds: those that target a single muscle, and those that involve an entire set of muscles. As an example of the first type of exercise we could take the biceps curl, and as an example of the second the lat pulldown. In the case of the first example, there is a minimal amount of assistance from surrounding muscles (the deltoids, the brachialis and triceps, and the forearm flexors) but the overwhelming majority of the muscular force is exerted by one muscle only, the biceps of the upper arm (biceps brachii). In the second case, however, the movement of the lat pulldown involves—in broadly equal measure, depending on the particular point in the range of movement—the muscles of the upper back from the deltoid inwards (teres major and minor, rhomboids, infraspinatus, trapezius) and of course the latissimus dorsi after which the exercise is named.

To take the second example first: what are the implications of performing lat pulldowns solely in the strongest part of the range? To grasp what is involved in this question, stand behind a trainer with particularly well-defined back muscles, and watch what happens as he or she performs a lat pulldown. You will note that the whole array of shoulder and upper- and middle-back muscles is involved, but in particular you will note the shifting 'muscle-landscape' of the back as the bar is pulled down to its lowest point and returned under control to its starting point. In effect, one muscle after another becomes the prime mover at successive points of the movement, as the position of the arms changes relative to the back. To understand the reason for this, you may care to refer to the table of muscles in *The Matrix Principle* (pp. 222 ff.), noting that each of the muscles involved has its own individual points of origin and insertion, which are brought closer together by its contraction. A whole series of contractions, each of a different muscle, is required to bring the arms down through the biomechanically complex lat pulldown movement.

To restrict lat pulldowns to the strongest (i.e. topmost) part of the total range of movement is thus to work only a part of this total interactive muscle system. This is not to say that the other muscles involved in the movement are left unused—all of them take on a certain amount of flexion, whatever the point in the range of movement—but they are never flexed to the maximum as happens when the full-range movement is performed.

Consider now the other kind of exercise we have mentioned—that which aims to target a single muscle rather than an interactive muscle-group. The example we quoted was the biceps curl. Again we can ask: what are the implications of performing biceps curls solely in the strongest part of the range? All experienced bodybuilders are aware that corrective exercises for those with a 'short' biceps (where there is a greater than average distance between the elbow joint and the curve of the flexed biceps) consist of working especially hard in the lower, or beginning, half of the curl movement. On the other hand, those trainers who find it hard to achieve a 'peak' on the biceps are usually advised to work especially on the upper half of the curl movement.

The reason for these differences relates to bunching patterns. If, for instance, we take the heaviest weight that we can curl and bring it to the midway position, we may assume that all relevant muscle fibres are fully recruited; if this is so, then how are we able to curl the weight another centimetre or two (as we can) towards the 'up' position? In fact, when we say that all 'relevant' muscle fibres are recruited, we are referring to those required to bring the weight to (or hold it in) a particular position. To bring it to another position is possible because other muscle fibres are still available to be brought into play. In other words, at any given point in the total curl movement, a certain *pattern* of muscle fibre activation is in force, and that pattern (known as the bunching pattern) is constantly changing as we perform the movement.

Bunching patterns

One of the most clearly observable illustrations of the effect of bunching patterns can be seen in the case of abdominal exercise. Those trainers (other than those lucky few who have naturally 'perfect' abs) who rely exclusively on abdominal crunches will find that they acquire good definition in the upper abs, but may well lack it completely in the lower abs, from the navel downwards. The usual answer to this problem is to ensure that, along with crunches, the trainer does at least the same number of reverse sit-ups or vertical bench leg raises. Yet when we speak of 'abs' in the plural we are often overlooking the fact that the abdominal wall is technically a single band of muscle rather than a set of discrete muscles. The view that to exercise a muscle is to exercise the *whole* muscle here shows its limitations, since in the case of the abdominal wall there may be a very clearly visible difference in development, depending on whether the muscle is 'hit' from the top (crunches) or the bottom (leg raises) of the single muscle band of which it is constituted. In effect, the crunch and the leg raise represent two kinds of part-rep—one from each end of the muscle—and the bunching pattern of the muscle is different in each case.

None of this is to deny the effectiveness of part-reps with heavy weight in the strongest part of the range, but rather to point out the limitations of restricting the range of movement. Two final examples may serve to illustrate this point. It is well attested, for instance, that a muscle is stronger in the eccentric (or negative) phase of contraction than in the concentric (or positive) phase, and that it is stronger still in the 'holding' or isometric position where the limb is held motionless. The 'heavy-weight' theory, if taken to its logical conclusion, would suggest that, rather than use the heaviest weights we can manage for a part-rep, we take the even heavier weight that we can hold in an isometric contraction. To return to the now familiar metaphor, the muscle does not 'know' what it is doing, only that it is being called upon to exert maximum force against the resistant object.

In fact, this is not merely a hypothetical scenario, but a training method which has been tried and extensively documented. The outcome is clear and well established—namely, that the muscle does indeed develop great strength in the position of the isometric holding, but *only in that position*. It may be extrapolated, then, that part-reps in the strongest part of the range do indeed develop strength in precisely that range of movement; but this would still leave wide open the question of whether the training effect would be equivalent to training in the full range as the 'whole muscle' hypothesis presupposes.

Lying Hamstring Flexes

The second example is taken from the world of sport and athletic training. For a long time, weights were little used in this area, but over the last generation or so the benefits of weight training have been increasingly recognised by sprinters, footballers and various other sports players who need to train for speed over short or middle distances and not merely train for strength and bulk. In general, this training has been found beneficial, but one persistent problem has remained—the prevalence of hamstring injuries, notwithstanding the widespread practice of standing or lying leg curls to build hamstring strength to the point where it more nearly approximates that of the quadriceps and thus to avoid the agonist/antagonist imbalance. Sports scientists today are increasingly recommending that sprinters supplement hamstring curls with lying hamstring flexes, and are finding consequently fewer injuries in this vulnerable area. Lying prone with ankles firmly anchored or held by a partner, the trainer lifts the upper part of the body from the floor with minimal or no assistance from the arms. In this position, the angle of the legs and body more closely replicates that in which hamstring injury is likely to be sustained on the track or field than does the less natural position of the leg curl. And yet the muscles involved (biceps femoris, semimembranosus and semitendinosus) may be as strongly worked in the leg curl as in the prone hamstring flex. The point, then, is that it is not the mere fact of working a muscle, but also the configuration in which it is worked, which may determine both strength and muscular development.

All of the above discussion provides confirmation of the usefulness of part-repetition training working across the entire range of movement, and not merely in one part of the range. While the latter can be highly effective, it is a training method relying on the use of heavy weights, whereas the alternative approach is to use lighter weights in ways which maximise their effect on the muscle system. Matrix repetitions deliberately target the *weakest* (as well as the strongest) part of the range of movement, stopping the weight at a number of points including those at which there is the least biomechanical assistance. In consequence the muscles have to work hardest, not receiving any of the momentum effect entailed in conventional repetitions. Some of the newer computer-controlled machines incorporate programs that utilise the Matrix 'sticking point' principle (including isometric pauses at the sticking points): these programs have been found, according to Dr Paul Ward, 'to develop maximal recruitment of all types of muscle fibers, which results in maximal increases in strength and hypertrophy'.[12] For those who can afford, or who have access to, such computerised-machine programs, this variation of Matrix-type exercise will undoubtedly be effective, although we believe that the same results can be obtained much less expensively (and with 36 different programs) in the standard Matrix routines.

So far, in this analysis, we have contrasted heavy weight with light-to-moderate weight—that is, anything up to 70% of a single rep maximum. Matrix training, however, tends to operate towards the lower end of this range, for the reason that it explicitly singles out the weakest parts of the range among the various end-points of repetitions—points at which the muscles have to work hardest to sustain even a moderate weight. Because it relies more on the repetition factor than on the weight factor to achieve maximum muscle fibre stimulation, it involves the cumulative fibre recruitment process as the means whereby, even with light weights, the hypertrophic effect is achieved. To refer to Matrix exercise as 'light-weight' exercise is, however, potentially misleading. Beginners, unfit exercisers, children and trainers in their advanced years can indeed use the Matrix method with very light weights and achieve a substantial challenge to the muscle system (without the concomitant risk of muscle injury, ligament tears and other potential problems of heavier-weight use to which such trainers are especially vulnerable). But more advanced trainers will find that, as they progress with Matrix training and their body adapts to it, they can use increasingly heavier weights—indeed, that they need to do so in order to achieve the same degree of challenge that they met with when they first discovered the Matrix system.

Although Matrix training, even in the case of advanced trainers (including elite athletes and professional bodybuilders), still uses lighter weights than conventional training, this is inherent in the system rather than because of a doctrinaire opposition to heavy weights. In other words, it is simply not physically possible to perform Matrix routines strictly, using the same weights one would normally use for conventional ten-repetition sets with standard pauses between them. In fact, we do not set out from the notion of *weight* at all—light or heavy—but rather from the notion of the particular Matrix technique performed *strictly*—that is, with strict form, and with the repetitions and specified pauses strictly adhered to. Trainers are advised to use the weight which will allow them to achieve this goal, and *not* to move to a heavier weight until they can perform the specified exercise strictly with their present training weight for that exercise. Very advanced trainers have been known to complete even some of the more demanding Matrix routines with weights approaching the upper end of the 'moderate' range, but their focus is always on completing the routine rather than on increasing the weight.

In summary, then, we can say that the training weight controversy is to at least some extent a false debate. In the first instance, we believe there is sufficient evidence to suggest that any categorical statement to the effect that *only* this type of weight, or that, will achieve optimum results is denying clearly established results to the contrary. And secondly, we have seen that a varied series of part repetitions (necessitating the use of relatively light weights) can play an important role in hitting the target muscle over the entire spectrum of its possible bunching patterns, including those which emerge only at the weakest points of the range.

In the next chapter, we shall go on to consider the further advantage offered by this type of training in effectively isolating the target muscles, and suggest some of the implications of this finding in terms of the mental input into the workout regime.

3   Isolation and awareness

One of the reasons for advocating moderate-weight alongside heavy-weight exercise is that, although the latter maximises the load on the muscle system, some of the effort can be dissipated and its effect negated by the spreading of the load among several extraneous muscles—primarily the synergist muscles—rather than concentrating on the prime mover. The heavier the weight, the more difficult it is to maintain strict form in order to isolate the muscle being targeted, for the reason that synergist (or assisting) muscles will be called upon to help stabilise the load. As Dr Michael Yessis has written:

> Electromyograph (EMG) studies reveal that isolation of minute muscle groups is indeed possible with low-intensity loading. However, if large loads are imposed on a particular muscle group, isolation becomes virtually impossible.
>
> Immediately after the load is applied, certain stabilising muscles become involved to ensure that specific joints remain stable, while the prime movers attempt to cope with the load. If the prime movers are inadequate to carry out the joint action, other muscles may be recruited to assist the primary muscles.
>
> In many cases the tension of the stabilisers or synergists will equal or exceed that of the prime mover. For example, during a heavy standing triceps pressdown, the abs, lats and erector spinae may be as strongly contracted as the triceps, even although this is supposed to be an exercise that isolates the triceps.[1]

Heavy weights are only one of the factors which make muscle isolation difficult. Where a group of muscles is involved interactively in an exercise movement, the effect of full repetitions may equally be to dissipate the load as momentum is relied upon to carry the weight through part of the movement. An example of this is the bench press, which involves the arms, shoulders and chest; it can easily be the case that the action of the anterior deltoid in moving the upper arm (adduction of the humerus) and that of the triceps in moving the lower arm (extension of the radius and ulna) provides a degree of momentum which takes the bar through the final third of the

'Imaging' Pec Deck Flyes so as to minimise the engagement of the deltoids.

movement, that in which the pecs are chiefly involved. To perform the bench press effectively as a pec exercise means ensuring that the upper part of the movement is not 'lost' in this way: part-repetitions in the upper area of the range may help prevent the exercise from becoming almost exclusively a deltoid and arm exercise.

Isolation and the mind

The problem of isolation is especially acute when the muscle being targeted is the weakest element of an interactive group. Here, the heavier the weight the greater the problem, since the tendency will be for the stronger or strongest muscle of the group to play an even greater role. This type of situation can be illustrated by looking at an exercise such as pec deck flyes. It is common for trainers to use a relatively heavy-weight adjustment on the pec deck, in the hope of getting a more thorough pec workout. The pectoral muscles, however—even in trainers with well developed pecs—are a relatively shallow band of muscle spread across the upper part of the thorax, and are comparatively weak (since the tasks they are called on by nature to perform are few in number and generally do not require great force). The deltoids, on the other hand, are not shallow bands but concentrated bunches of muscle capable of exerting considerable force and frequently acting as prime mover in shifting the body or resisting opposing forces. When pec deck flyes are attempted with a weight that is too heavy to be shifted by the pecs without assistance, the inevitable outcome is that the much stronger deltoids take over and the exercise becomes an anterior deltoid rather than pectoral developer.

This is not to say that reducing the weight will, of itself, guarantee the isolation of the target muscle(s). Pec deck flyes, for example, even when performed with light weights, are still engaging an interactive set of muscles in which the deltoids may predominate over the pectorals as prime mover. How, then, is the trainer able to use the exercise in order to isolate the pecs and thus work them to the maximum? Many trainers find that an effective method is a variant of the technique described in *The Matrix Principle* (pp. 122–4) which we have referred to as 'imaging'. In the present case, the trainer first performs a few reps of the exercise in strict form but with *no weight* (i.e. the arms are not held behind the pec deck pads, but simply perform the 'hugging' movement relative to the body). In the earlier volume, we indicated some of the uses of the imaging technique, including that of simulating the effect of a heavier weight than that being used. Here, however, the point of the technique is to gain the 'feel' of the movement when performed optimally, so as to be able to transfer this 'feel' to the actual training situation.

In the case of pec deck flyes, it is crucial to shift the load from the delts to the pecs. The trainer, therefore, 'images' the movement by squeezing or contracting the pecs with no weight resistance, bringing the arms forward by so doing. It may take a few repetitions to establish the feel of the movement, but the trainer will soon become accustomed to thinking: 'I am contracting the pecs, and this brings my arms forward', instead of (subconsciously) thinking: 'I am bringing my arms forward to move the pec deck pads closer together'. In the latter case, the almost inevitable result of the mental concentration on the arms is the focusing of effort on the shoulders (i.e. on the anterior head of the deltoid as adductor of the humerus). Having established the feeling of doing the exercise *by using the pecs*, the trainer then moves to the pec deck and, with relatively light weights, transfers the pec-contracting movement to the flyes. To the casual observer, the trainer appears to be doing the exercise no differently than if the shoulders were the prime mover; the trainer, however, will feel from the increased pump in the pecs just how fundamentally the driving force has changed.

There is nothing particularly new about this technique and its variations, which have been described under various names as instructors and training writers have sought to devise methods of exploiting mental concentration and mental targeting of particular muscle groups. Dr Daniel McCarthy and Nancy McCarthy, for example, have described what they refer to as the Focused Intensity Visualisation (FIV) method of training—a five-step method of mentally approaching the weight workout which covers most of its psychological aspects from motivation and goal setting to concentration and mental rehearsal of each movement in strict form.[2] From a slightly different perspective, Dr John Tristany has written on particular applications of psychophysiology (a term introduced in the 1970s to refer to areas of psychosomatic medicine) in which hypnosis is used to foster the conscious voluntary control of internal glandular and neuromuscular responses. This process, too, involves constructing a mental picture of the physical movement as a prelude to more sophisticated techniques using internal perceptions as conditioned stimuli.[3]

The growth of the discipline of sports psychology has in fact provided serious sporting trainers with an impressive array of techniques for mental focusing—as well as for improving motivation, coping with stress, goal setting and attainment, and the like. Many of these techniques will be known to advanced bodybuilders and athletes, especially those who are used to training with heavy weights and to employing the 'psyching-up' methods used by powerlifters and Olympic weightlifters before a heavy lift. The techniques mentioned above, among other similar approaches to the psychology of training, are in our opinion worthy of attention by trainers wishing to maximise the effectiveness of their workout, even if a certain amount of experimentation may be required before finding the particular method best suited to the individual trainer's psychological make-up.

Focusing and visualisation techniques are being constantly refined and can be highly effective. Many of them go back to discoveries made in the 1950s and 1960s, which revealed for example that mental practice in throwing darts at a target—whereby the person sits for a period each day in front of the target, and *imagines* throwing darts at it—improves aim as much as actually throwing darts.[4] The 'mental rehearsal' technique soon had advocates in a wide variety of fields—from the celebrated pianist Artur Schnabel to the champion golfer Ben Hogan—and even today the proponents of mental imagery and visual rehearsal point to training effects as powerful as those of actual training. Michael Hutchinson has written that through the use of visualisation techniques in a float tank, 'bodybuilders . . . find that they can mentally run through an entire workout with total clarity in just a few minutes, and their bodies seem to respond with growth, as they would in an actual workout'.[5]

Rather than suggest yet another mental concentration technique in competition with others, our aim in this section is to examine the basis on which such techniques are ultimately founded—the mind–body connection—and to suggest why Matrix training is especially compatible with any visualisation or mental imaging method which seeks to make the training experience an engagement of more than simply the physical faculties.

In the case of light- and moderate-weight exercise, the type of mental engagement which is particularly useful is not only different from the psyching-up of the heavyweight lifter, but also involves a degree of muscle awareness and control which is actually inhibited by an exclusive reliance on heavy weights. It depends, in fact, on exploiting to the maximum the techniques of imaging and visualisation we referred to above, and on using our body's own feedback in order to increase our consciousness of muscular activity. Most people have a general idea of what is meant by feedback (and its derivative, biofeedback), but it would be useful at this stage to give a brief overview of these terms and the phenomena to which they refer, before going on to indicate some of the ways in which they can be incorporated into the training regime.

Feedback and biofeedback

The term 'feedback' was first used by radio pioneers in the early 1900s to describe a process which they defined as 'the return to input of some of the output of a system'.[6] Feedback, it was discovered, could help to control a system by reinserting into it the results of its own past performance. While this technical sense continues in modern times ('a control system which tends to maintain a prescribed relationship of one system variable to another by comparing functions of these variables and using the differences as a means of control'),[7] the term has also developed a metaphorical and more popular sense. When politicians ask for 'feedback' from voters or a manufacturer seeks 'feedback' from customers, the term tends to mean little more than 'response' or 'reaction' rather than implying that the response or reaction will necessarily be used to determine the politician's future actions or the manufacturer's product development. Strictly, however, the notion of using information as feedback entails the positive role of this information in directing future action. While we tend not to use the term in relation to the everyday business of living, it is actually the simple motor tasks we perform at every waking moment that provide the most readily grasped examples of feedback. Hugh Downs puts it as follows:

> I reach for a light switch. My eyes inform me when my hand is close and because of this information I put the brakes on my arm muscles so as to arrive at the light switch without crashing into it. Or groping in the dark, my sense of touch will send back the signal of contact with the switch and appropriate instructions will be issued by the brain to the hand.[8]

This is an example of kinaesthetic feedback, which we constantly use in the performance of motor tasks and the learning of new motor skills, monitoring each stage of the movement to minimise and correct errors as we go along.

Biofeedback is a particular kind of feedback. Defined by Barbara Brown as 'the feedback of biological information to the person whose biology it is',[9] it can perhaps best be thought of as using information, not from the external world, but from our own internal world, as part of the control system governing that internal world. The real breakthrough in this area was made in the 1960s by scientists working in the field of psychosomatic processes. At the Rockefeller University in New York, psychologist Dr Neal

Miller was experimenting with conditioned learning techniques. As Locke and Colligan have recounted, Miller:

> . . . managed to train a group of rats to raise or lower their heart rate or blood pressure on command by sending a pulse of electricity to the 'pleasure centers' of their brains. In time the rats became so skilled that they could relax or control specific muscles of their intestines and even control the flow of blood to one or both of their ears. In one swoop those mysterious feats of the yogis—raising the temperature of one hand or racing or slowing the beat of their hearts—did not seem so mysterious.[10]

It was not long before these techniques were being tested on humans, and by the early 1970s there was a major efflorescence of books, articles and popular discussion on the potential benefits of biofeedback techniques in controlling internal human functions and promoting health. Patients were hooked up to equipment that amplified one or more internal body signals and translated them into clearly visible or audible form: a flashing light, perhaps, or a tone. The person linked up to the biofeedback device then aimed to modify his or her body activities by listening to the tone or watching the light.

It was not long before writers on biofeedback technique such as Karlins and Andrews were assuring readers that 'once a person can "see" his heartbeats or "hear" his brain waves, he has the information he needs to begin controlling them'.[11] The prospect of using biofeedback techniques to eliminate depression, psychosomatic disease, high blood pressure, drug dependence and a host of other physical and emotional problems led to high expectations as to the therapeutic value of the technique, although very few of these were actually realised. In some areas, such as cardiac arrhythmias, migraine headaches and neuromuscular disorders, the accumulated evidence of therapeutic value appears to be more favourable, but in others the effects often appear variable, short-lived or uncertain.[12]

What is the relevance of biofeedback to weight training? To answer this question will require fairly detailed discussion, but we can begin by considering the more common 'kinaesthetic feedback' mentioned above. Here, the clues provided by the external environment are used to direct our motor system in performing common tasks: indeed, all muscular activity and all learning of motor skills involve some form of kinaesthetic feedback. Restricting our discussion to the activity of the muscles, we shall look first at the neuromuscular information loop to which we referred earlier. A convenient starting point to adopt is the action of lifting a weight, which necessarily begins with the 'perception' of the limbs that there is a weight which resists them, and that to lift it will require muscular engagement. To give a full account of the complex set of processes involved is outside our present scope, but we may note in passing that the initial perception process may involve a variety of factors such as vision (the weight *looks* heavy) and previous knowledge (we know that the weight has 100 lb marked on it and we have a good idea of how heavy that is). To some extent, we use the process known as 'feedforward' in preparing to lift the weight: technically defined as 'the provision of predictive information about impending changes in regulated variables',[13] feedforward can be broadly described in the present context as expectation and anticipation directing the setting of our mental and kinetic functions.

Feeling the weight

Omitting extra-muscular factors for the purpose of this simplified discussion, we can begin with the pressure receptors which tell us the resistance of the weight to the muscles of the limb. These receptors, probably consisting of Golgi tendon organs and muscle spindles (perhaps in combination),[14] signal the adjustment of force necessary to move the weight. Once movement has begun, a further process comes into play whereby muscle length and limb position are constantly monitored to compare actual length with instructed length and the difference is used as an error signal to generate a correcting movement. This process will be familiar to anyone with even an elementary knowledge of control engineering or systems theory: in summary form, it means that an error between the intended state and actual state of a system is picked up and rectified by a correcting signal. The difference between states is referred to as a 'gain', and where a small error is rectified by a powerful correcting signal, the system is said to have a high loop gain. In this present case, the gain of the proprioceptive receptors in the muscle system is constantly being modified, as our sensory input (how far the arms have travelled, as determined by their 'feel' and, in some cases, our vision of them) is compared with how far we are instructing them to travel; the use of a correcting signal based on loop gain to vary the muscle contraction and arm position as necessary, is basically a simple feedback process.[15]

It was stated above that this is a simplified account. A fuller analysis would need to refer to receptors outside the muscles themselves—mechanoreceptors in the deep tissue close to the joints and in the joints themselves, as well as various other points on the moto-neuronal pathway. For our present purpose, however, it will suffice to concentrate on the motor unit itself. In the discussion above, we indicated that incoming signals from the various receptors are processed in such a way as to modify the muscular action and control its succeeding movements. But what is it that does the controlling? Physiologists describe this controlling mechanism as the *motor servo*. A servo mechanism usually takes the form of a goal-seeking device— a guidance system which steers its way towards a goal by responding to feedback. Examples of servo systems are the self-guided torpedo or the interceptor missile. In addition to the propulsion system required to drive the device, it needs to be equipped with 'sense organs' which respond to feedback signals: if feedback is positive, no correcting action is necessary; if feedback is negative, a correcting mechanism comes into play.

In the case of the motor servo, the propulsion system is under the control of the nervous system, the muscle receptors acting as 'sense organs'. A concise (if somewhat technical) description of its function is that given by Houk and Rymer :

> It consists of a mechanical portion (an individual muscle and the load upon which it acts) and a neuroregulatory portion (the set of autogenic reflex pathways) . . . The signals traversing these pathways originate from muscle stretch receptors, they are integrated by a neural network organised predominantly at a segmental level in the spinal cord, and the resultant electromotor output returns in motor axons to the same muscle from which the afferent signals originated. Thus autogenetic circuits are actually local feedback loops, which apparently function to regulate the mechanical variables monitored by the various muscle receptors. These variables are muscle length (and its derivatives) sensed by muscle spindle receptors, and muscle force or tension sensed by Golgi tendon organs.[16]

The motor servo functions, then, as a processor of motor commands that are sent to it from other regions of the nervous system in ensembles of nerve fibres. Its role is to translate central motor commands into changes in muscle length and force, taking into account the properties and behaviour of the mechanical load itself. Houk and Rymer distinguish this role from that of the central nervous system (CNS), their hypothesis being that:

> . . . the CNS controls movements by setting central motor commands to particular constant values and by then letting the particular modulations in torque required to execute the movement evolve as a natural consequence of mechanical and reflex interactions at the level of the motor servo.[17]

This suggests that we may almost think of the motor servo as a kind of miniature, localised equivalent of the CNS, which does the detailed work while the central nervous system itself gives overall general commands.

Whether central or peripheral, these systems operate in such a way as to create an 'internal neural correlate' of any motor signal. In over-simple, but not entirely misleading, terms, we can say that for any action of the motor system, there is a counterpart (or 'correlate') of that action within the nervous system: other terms with similar meanings used by physiologists are 'command collaterals', 'corollary discharges' and 'efference copies', all of which refer to consequences or corollaries of the motor commands, modifications within the nervous system arising from, or together with, these commands. The standard reference on these phenomena is Professor D. I. McCloskey's entry in the authoritative *Handbook of Physiology*,[18] and it may be helpful, in providing a simplified account for our present purposes, to refer to three revealing examples quoted by McCloskey to indicate the existence and action of this neural system:

1. *The Phantom Limb.* McCloskey reports that, in about 95% of amputation cases, the patient experiences the illusion that the amputated limb still 'exists' and can change its perceived position in space in response to

motor commands dispatched to it. That this sensation is not caused by peripheral inputs (e.g. from the muscles that normally move the amputated part) but may be generated, or at least maintained, by nervous activity wholly internal to the central nervous system, has been shown experimentally. There is thus what can be called an 'internal representation of position' or 'body scheme' which can be awakened even after the removal of the relevant body part.[19]

2. *Paralysis*. This is in some ways the reverse of the phantom limb phenomenon. Whereas in the case of the phantom limb we can feel the sensation of movement in the absence of an actual limb, in the case of paralysis the limb is still present but we are unable to feel the sensation of movement even when it is moving (e.g. being manipulated). In the case of paralysis (at least of the limb and trunk musculature), motor commands are unable to evoke sensations of innervation in the form of sensations of movement.[20]

3. *High-frequency vibration*. McCloskey reports that when high-frequency vibration is applied through the skin over a muscle or its tendon, the vibrated muscle contracts involuntarily: this 'tonic vibration reflex' is usually attributed to excitation of the primary endings of muscle spindles. What is interesting, however, is that the subject whose muscle is vibrated experiences an illusion of movement at the joint about which the vibrated muscle operates. This illusion, however, does not occur in the case of a strongly contracting muscle, suggesting that 'some central process sorts and transmits only the kinesthetically significant portion of receptor firing'.[21]

The three examples quoted by McCloskey are revealing because they indicate cases wherein what is actually happening to our muscles is out of step with what we *feel* is happening to them. Such findings, and others of a similar nature, lead to the postulation of a 'correlate' (or counterpart) of the motor system within the nervous system; whereas the two systems normally work in concert (so that what we *feel* is happening to our muscles is what is *actually* happening to them), the occasional disparities quoted above remind us that we are actually involved with two systems which 'talk to each other' as it were, and that the message sometimes becomes garbled.

A final example, which brings us even closer to the world of weight training, relates to the sensation of heaviness. McCloskey, again, points out that if one carries a load for long enough to cause the muscles supporting that load to become fatigued, then one notices that the load seems to grow heavier:

This phenomenon can be demonstrated objectively by asking a subject to support a weight with one arm for a prolonged period. The subject chooses at various intervals through that period weights that seem as heavy as the continuously supported one. These matching weights are lifted with the corresponding muscles of the opposite arm and are supported only intermittently, so that this arm does not become fatigued. The subject

Sharon Laura demonstrates Seated Hammer Curls.

chooses successively larger weights to match the one borne by the gradually fatiguing arm, showing that the perceived heaviness of the continuously supported weight does indeed increase.[22]

McCloskey devotes lengthy discussion to the question of whether the sensation of heaviness is generated by sensory receptors (i.e. at the periphery, in the muscles themselves) or as a result of effort employed (i.e. centrally, in the motor command system). His conclusion is, in essence, that it is the latter—the motor command system—that 'perceives' heaviness. When, for example, the antagonist of a contracting muscle is vibrated, the weight will suddenly feel heavier even though it remains the same.

To put it bluntly, if somewhat crudely: while heaviness is in the weight, the *sensation* of heaviness is in the mind. To return once more to our recurring theme, the muscle does not 'know' how heavy the weight is. All it knows, and can report to the central nervous system, is its own state of tension, which the central nervous system uses as an 'event marker', a part of the total array of information which indicates whether the desired task has or has not been completed. In the case of perceived heaviness, as in the other examples quoted above, there can sometimes be a disparity or disproportion between the actual situation or state of the muscle and the perceived situation or the sensation that we feel.

Mind over muscle

In all the cases quoted above, it can be said that it was the neurotransmitting element of the servo system that was somehow 'tricked': the information reaching the central nervous system was flawed or illusory. In most cases, however, the higher intelligence—armed with other (e.g. visual) clues—perceives these illusions for what they are. The amputee can feel the phantom limb, but does not believe that it has been miraculously restored to the body; the quadriplegic can see the paralysed limb, and does not believe it has disappeared simply because it cannot be felt; and so on. At the other end of the scale, the muscles themselves have no intelligence and can only respond to the commands given them. The question, then, is whether we can send messages from the central nervous system to the muscle servo system which can actually 'trick' the latter into giving the muscles commands that will make them behave *as if* they were called upon to shift a load requiring a higher degree of fibre recruitment.

We might preface our response to this question by the observation that, even in the most strenuous workout, we tend to use only a part of the total reserve of strength and force of which the muscle system is capable. There are no doubt good reasons for this: nature has designed the muscle system in such a way that it will, if possible, avoid injuring itself. It seems likely that muscle fatigue has precisely this role, preventing us from overtaxing the muscles and possibly injuring them. The role of the servo system in signalling fatigue is thus important, although it is worth noting that it is possible to bypass the control mechanism in certain cases. Under hypnosis, for example, or when confronted by a moment of life-threatening crisis, people have often been known to perform feats of strength of which they would not 'normally' (i.e. when under rational control) have been capable.[23]

We shall explore this phenomenon further in a moment. For the present, however, let us return to the question posed above: is it possible to 'trick' the muscles by an exercise of the will, by sending them the message that the weight is heavier than it actually is? We have seen from the example just quoted that in fact this process is happening all the time, as one repetition succeeds another: at each repetition, more and more muscle fibres are recruited (which is why one single repetition is ineffective) and the weight seems heavier, so that we need to employ more and more effort to finish the set. Yet in fact, the weight is no heavier at the end of the set than at the beginning: what has changed is that the fatigue response has intervened, making the weight *seem* heavier. At the same time, because it *seems* heavier, more and more muscle fibre is recruited in order to shift it.

In this example, admittedly, it is the fatigue response that 'tricks' the muscle into reacting as though the weight was heavier than it is, and the question is still left open whether the same effect can be achieved by the exercise of the will. This is the process attempted in one of the uses of the 'imaging' technique described in *The Matrix Principle*: the trainer holds a light weight, but 'tells' the muscles that it is actually a heavy weight, and performs the exercise accordingly. Anyone who has tried this will attest to the fact that—perhaps after a little practice—it is quite easy to give this message to the muscles, in such a way that the weights actually do *feel* heavier than they are. That is not, however, the crucial issue: the question is not whether the weights simply *feel* heavier—as if we were dealing with one of those illusions such as the phantom limb—but whether the muscles in fact respond as if the weights were heavier.

In the case of the phantom limb, we saw that the servo could be the sender of a false message delivered 'upstream'—that is, it reports to the central nervous system what is not really the case (the existence of a limb and its muscular activity). In the case of fatigue, the servo sends a false message 'downstream'—that is, it reports to the muscles that the weight is growing heavier, and they respond accordingly by recruiting more muscle fibre. Confirmation of this 'downstream' signalling effect may be found in recent research by Gandevia et al., who deliberately paralysed themselves with a drug, then tried to contract paralysed muscles. What they found was that, although (for obvious reasons) the paralysed muscles did not move, both blood pressure and heart rate increased.[24] The experiment indicates that the central nervous system's commands to the muscles are enough to create a strong, appropriate reaction in the body's circuitry system—which is, in effect, 'tricked' into behaving as though there were a load on the muscles whereas the 'load' is purely in the mind.

This research bears out observations made over many years on hypnotised subjects. In his valuable book on self-image, *Psycho-Cybernetics*, Dr Maxwell Maltz has written:

> If a good hypnotic subject is told that he is at the North Pole he will not only shiver and *appear* to be cold, his body will react just as if he were cold and goose pimples will develop. The same phenomenon has been demonstrated on wide awake college students by asking them to *imagine* that one hand is immersed in ice water. Thermometer readings show that the temperature does drop in the 'treated' hand. Tell a hypnotised subject that your finger is a red hot poker and he will not only grimace with pain at your touch, but his cardiovascular and lymphatic systems will react just as if your finger were a red hot poker and produce inflammation and perhaps a blister on the skin. When college students, wide awake, have been told to *imagine* that a spot on their foreheads was hot, temperature readings have shown an actual increase in skin temperature.[25]

The nervous system, Maltz points out, cannot tell the difference between an imagined experience and a 'real' experience. In either case, it reacts automatically to information given to it from the forebrain, acting in accordance with what the mind thinks or imagines to be true. It is not necessary, he argues, actually to *believe* the experience to be true: the nervous system 'cannot tell the difference between an actual experience and one that is vividly imagined. If we picture ourselves performing in a certain manner, it is nearly the same as the actual performance'.[26]

While imaging or visualisation is not an integral part of Matrix exercise, it makes a particularly good adjunct to it. This is because the techniques of Matrix training are already taking advantage of the ability of the nerve-to-muscle signalling system to provoke maximum muscle fibre activation from minimal weight input. By the use of multiple repetitions, Matrix (like conventional training) exploits the capacity of the moto-neuron system to signal an ever greater response with each repetition; but by favouring the weakest points of the range, and by continually varying the repetition-type so that the bunching pattern is constantly altered, a greater variety of muscle fibres is called upon than in standard repetitions which repeat exactly the same movement. In this way, the Matrix method goes further than conventional training towards exploiting those reserves of muscular capacity which are latent within the body's muscle system but hardly ever tapped. To the extent that mental focusing can (as it were) persuade the nervous system to release more of those reserves by increasing the stimulation of muscle fibre beyond the physical demands imposed by the load, it can only add further to the effectiveness of Matrix training.

Earlier in this chapter, we asked what was the relevance of biofeedback to the weight-training process. In setting out to answer this question, we have concentrated on mind-to-muscle and muscle-to-mind signals, our aim being both to describe some of the mechanisms involved and to suggest ways in which trainers can use their mental input (i.e. the command process) to influence muscle fibre recruitment. To be most effective, such training methods need to make active use of feedback techniques of the kind we described earlier—and in particular, to move beyond kinaesthetic feedback into the realm of biofeedback. We have quoted a number of examples to show how the trainer can use light weights (or even 'imaging' without weights) to pinpoint mentally the target muscle being exercised. The biofeedback technique involves, first, feeling the muscle contraction 'from the inside', as it were, and, second, mentally *using* that contraction to perform the exercise rather than mentally focusing on the kinaesthetic feedback provided by the moving of the limb. In this process, as with all biofeedback experience, we are gaining progressively greater control over our body's processes—in this case, the voluntary contraction of targeted muscles.

Muscle control and body control

Voluntary control of the muscle system can best be envisaged as a kind of continuum. At the one end are those cases in which control is deficient or impossible: a muscle spasm due to illness or disability, for example, or the celebrated 'knee-jerk' reaction (in the literal rather than the metaphorical sense). In these cases, as in that quoted earlier of the high-frequency vibration of a muscle or its tendon, we have the production of a stimulus independent of the conscious will, whether the source of that stimulus is inside the body or in the outside world. At the other end of the spectrum, we can place some of the more spectacular demonstrations of muscle control that have been associated with advanced practitioners of hatha yoga—in

The Side Chest pose performed by a master, Professional Mr Universe John Terilli.

particular the control of the abdominal muscles, which can be sucked in to a remarkable degree, made to quiver, or contracted in an amazing variety of patterns. Somewhere between these two extremes lie the myriad physical actions we all perform as we go about the normal business of daily living.

Close to the end of the scale occupied by the more accomplished yogis, we may place those bodybuilders whose competition posing routines involve a high degree of voluntary muscle control. Some skilled contestants can achieve impressive and even spectacular effects, creating a cavernous abdominal vacuum, making their pecs jump up and down either together or individually, or performing various other feats of posing skill which add to the 'show business' element of competition. But even at the strictly sporting level, muscle control is a vital ability for the competitive bodybuilder. Although most of the standard repertoire of poses involve the display of mass and definition by means of the tension of one muscle group against another, it is necessary in certain poses to learn how to flex particular muscle groups without the benefit of other, opposing groups.

An example may perhaps make this distinction clearer. In the Side Chest pose, for instance, the biceps nearer the judges and audience is fully flexed as that arm is bent at the elbow and the wrist or hand tensed against the hand of the opposite arm, which is exerting downward pressure against the upward biceps flex. The leg nearer the audience is slightly bent at the knee, the downward pressure on the toes and ball of the foot having the effect of contracting the calf muscle (the gastrocnemius) while the thigh of the bent leg is usually held pressed against the opposing leg to bring out the separation of the external vastus. In this pose, the flexion of the main muscle-groups is achieved by tensing them against the resistance of other muscles or an external object (the floor). Contrast this with the Abs and Thighs pose, where the competitor must bring out the definition of the quadriceps group in the upper leg as well as that of the abdominals *simply by flexing* these muscles—that is, without the resistance offered by another body part or external object.

To perform the latter kind of pose may not sound difficult, but in fact it is a skill which some bodybuilders—even those who would score well on the criteria of muscularity, symmetry, proportion, definition and the like—find extremely hard to master. Some discover that they have no problem flexing the abs, but are unable to bring out the muscles of the leg when it is held straight; others find that they can flex one leg but not the other; while still other aspiring competitors may be able to flex the legs but cannot voluntarily bring out the lats in the Rear Lat Spread pose. To acquire these capabilities is no easy task for some bodybuilders, while others find that it presents no problems at all. In our training manual for competition bodybuilders, *The Posing Handbook* (Bantam, Sydney, 1995), we have provided practical advice on the means of acquiring those posing skills which rely on voluntary muscle control rather than resistance. Without retracing that ground here, it is relevant to the present discussion to mention the use of feedback techniques in teaching the body to develop this ability to flex the muscles without an external source of tension.

The technique involved is, in fact, a fairly elementary form of biofeedback. It will be recalled that an essential element in biofeedback training is a signalling device (often a light or a buzzer) which indicates when the intended biological response has been achieved. In the present case, the signalling device is replaced by a mirror, which the trainer uses in practising the poses. It may take only a few training sessions, or quite a large number, before the learner is able to produce a visible flexion simply by telling the relevant muscles to contract voluntarily so that they stand out in full definition (for example, so that the separation of the rectus femoris from the surrounding vastus muscles can be clearly seen by the trainer looking into the mirror). Once this effect is visibly achieved—even if only to a slight degree at first—the trainer must then close his or her eyes, and concentrate on the 'feel' in the muscles when they are held in this position. This process will need to be repeated, and in some cases repeated a large number of times, in order to reinforce the message: whether slowly or rapidly, the trainer is able to move more and more easily into the flexed position, checking in the mirror that it has been achieved, then closing the eyes to 'fix' the sensation mentally. Finally, the trainer must learn to become less and less dependent on the mirror, by means of flexing with the eyes closed (relying totally on the feel of the muscles) and opening them only to check that the look of the pose is correct.

Towards body control

The above technique relies, as we have said, on an elementary form of biofeedback. Its relevance is not only to training in the sport of competition bodybuilding, but also more generally to the techniques of muscle control which can be used in the normal weight workout. At a much more sophisticated level, muscle control via biofeedback has been studied experimentally, confirming the examples we have cited above and revealing the surprising extent to which bodily processes can be brought under conscious control.

Most of the standard biofeedback devices are used to record processes of the autonomic nervous system, that part of the nervous system which supplies tissues and organs not normally considered to be under voluntary control; some work has also been done, however, on other parts of the nervous system including the brain and spinal cord (the central nervous system). Among the instruments used for these experiments, we may list:

- the electrocardiogram (ECG), which monitors heart beat;
- the electroencephalograph (EEG), which monitors activity originating in the brain;
- the thermistor, for taking the temperature of local areas of skin;
- the skin resistance meter, which gives a direct measure of arousal; and
- the electromyograph (EMG), which measures impulses associated with muscle tension.

Some ECG experiments have been claimed to enable subjects to regulate their heartbeats, while EEG experiments have been cited in which subjects can control their 'brain waves' or brain rhythms (changing the latter's frequencies from, say, the 13–26 Hz or beta range to the 8–13 Hz or alpha range). Among the experimental data, those with the most relevance here have to do with the EMG studies carried out by the physiologist John Basmajian.[27]

Basmajian used an electromyograph with extremely small sensing electrodes (25 μmm in diameter) to demonstrate that a subject can be trained to control the operation of a single muscle cell. This was an altogether remarkable finding, not only because of the extraordinarily small size of an individual cell, but also because of the organisation of the neuromuscular system. As Brown has put it:

> The voluntary control of a single cell is all the more incredible when one considers the complexity and extensiveness of the neural connections each cell can make with various parts of the cerebral cortex and other parts of the central nervous system. It is estimated that some 600 or more nerve fibres make connection with and influence each motor nerve cell. These in

turn may connect with the interconnections of nearly 10 billion brain cells in one hemisphere.[28]

Basmajian began by linking his monitoring and recording apparatus to the muscle cell (e.g. a cell of the abductor pollicis brevis in the hand), the impaled cell being detected through its discharge and recovery of electrical energy. In the experiment, the electrical response of the cells innervated by a single motor cell in the spinal cord was recorded on an oscilloscope. Each muscle cell has its own individual pattern or 'signature' which will show up on an oscilloscope screen and can also be represented by an audible pattern of 'bleeps'. The latter are simply translations into sounds of the electrical changes constantly taking place in the nerve muscle systems.

What Basmajian found was that normal human subjects could learn to pick up the individual rhythms or patterns of the electric charges carrying the messages of the motor nerve to the muscle cells, and after a short period of training (as little as 15–20 minutes) could cause one or other of these patterns to show up on the oscilloscope screen or register audibly as a recognisable pattern of bleeps. In effect, this means Basmajian's subjects were able to isolate one motor unit from the population of perhaps 100 to 200 which were within the area of pick-up of the electrodes, and could control it voluntarily.

The relevance of these experiments to weight training may not be immediately apparent, the more so as other experiments in muscle feedback voluntary control have shown that the most easily controlled muscle cells are those within muscles that we are used to controlling in daily life—such as those of the hands, feet and face—whereas, say, the muscles of the chest or back are more difficult to control.[29] It may be that this difference in response is to some extent inherent in the neuromuscular configuration of the various areas of the body: there are certainly differences from one muscle group to another in the number of muscle fibres activated by individual motor units, the muscles involved in fine movements having as few as five muscle fibres per nerve fibre while larger coarse-acting muscles may have as many as 2000.[30] It has been suggested, however, that the difference in ease of control may equally have to do with the extent to which the muscle groups involved have already learnt to respond in this way. As Brown puts it:

> . . . The cell or system always has some background information, and the more it has, the more quickly it learns something new. The motor nerve cells in the spinal cord which have had more 'training', particularly those in most frequent 'willed' or aware operations (fingers, arms, noses, etc.) are brought under voluntary control much more quickly than those supplying nerve messages to the large supporting muscles that are used in rather simple movements.[31]

To the extent that the latter hypothesis is correct, it should be possible for us to use biofeedback techniques to achieve a much greater degree of control over the activity of our large muscle groups than we normally seek to attempt.

In summary, these findings would seem to provide confirmation of what has been said above concerning the usefulness of mental imaging techniques as part of the weight workout. Those bodybuilders with extensive posing experience frequently attest to the value of posing practice itself as a form of muscle training. Some top professional bodybuilders are known to spend almost as much time on posing practice as they do on their weights in the gym—not so much in order to perfect their posing routine (although this is part of the reason) as to gain the benefit, in terms of visible muscularity, that only voluntary flexing can bring. Like any other learnt skill, the voluntary muscle flex needs constant reinforcement if it is to be maintained at a high level of competence; but, more than this, the ability to make one muscle stand out from others (muscle separation) often cannot be acquired from weight training alone but can come only from the mastery of muscle control techniques, for the reason that weight training uses the tension of an external object or resistant limb rather than the mere exercise of the will in order to produce muscular flexion. Thus, while leg extensions may develop the muscles of the quadriceps, only the voluntary flexing of the leg (without the resistance of a weight or another limb) will make the quadriceps stand out in full definition when the legs are held straight.

Not all the readers of this book will be interested in taking up competition bodybuilding or wish to develop posing skills. The examples quoted above are intended primarily as illustrations of a principle which goes well beyond the muscle control of the accomplished poser. The latter is chosen simply as an example—and one to which all weight trainers can easily relate—of the intimate connection between mind and body of which voluntary muscle control provides a telling demonstration. In the earlier sections on imaging, we have suggested ways in which this mental control of the muscles can be translated into the actual training situation, as the trainer—using his or her knowledge of anatomy to target the muscles involved in a particular exercise—concentrates mentally on those muscles so as to suppress the involvement of synergists. In this way, as the muscles learn to respond more and more effectively to control signals, we can add significantly to the effectiveness of the workout by eliminating the dilution of effort which results from the involvement of extraneous muscles.

4 Health and the mind: the Matrix approach

The mind in control

The point was made in the previous chapter that the targeting technique is not a necessary part of Matrix weight training, but that it is highly compatible with it. As a light- to moderate-weight system that relies on increasing intensity rather than heavier weight as a measure of progress, Matrix leaves much more scope for the mind to control the body's reactions than do conventional techniques in which muscular response is dictated solely by the load. It is worth adding, however, that mental control is a technique which is especially compatible with the Matrix *system*, viewed not simply as a weight training method but also as the basis of a holistic approach to exercise, fitness and health.

In this chapter, we shall explore some of the wider ramifications of this approach, especially in relation to the role of the mind in promoting physical health. In this respect, a holistic approach is perhaps best understood as the opposite of a 'compartmentalising' view of the human organism—that is, the view that the various aspects of our existence (physical, mental, emotional, spiritual) are entirely separate from one another and do not interact. The corollary of the latter view is that there is no single, organising principle which controls this assemblage of parts all acting independently of one another. On the contrary, what brings together the various components of the Matrix system into a coherent ensemble of interactive elements is in fact the notion of being *in control*—that is, of using the physical and mental resources with which we are endowed rather than surrendering control of them to forces outside ourselves.

A case in point is our vigorous opposition to the drug culture and, in particular, to the use of anabolic steroids and similar substances by weight trainers and bodybuilders. It is not only the proven health risks of steroid and HGH use, or even the ethical issues raised by drug taking in the world of sport, which lead us to put forward Matrix training as an alternative to artificial growth-enhancing substances, it is also that the mentality they foster—the quick fix, 'magic bullet' approach to altering the state of the body—ultimately involves the handing over of control to forces outside ourselves. The sheer unpredictability of the effect of steroids, including their psychotropic (mind or mood-altering) effect on certain individuals, would be in our view sufficient reason to avoid their use irrespective of their adverse physical consequences. The Matrix system is based on the principle that not only a healthy physical lifestyle, but also a healthier mental outlook, will result from the more effective utilisation of our natural capacities. As Professor Ronald Laura has written elsewhere:

> When all is said, it would appear that the doping problem in sport is a facet of the drug problem in society. Continually seeking instant gratification, we have as a society turned to technological innovation, wherever it is found, as a short-cut to achieve our goals. In regard to drugs we have been seduced by the power of the pill as if the medicine cabinet was an armoury of magic bullets, to be used against the enemies of hard work and persistent effort. We have become progressively distracted as a culture from the way of nature to the way of the chemist. We have structured our society, our institutions and our technological innovations in ways which reinforce our craving for instant satisfaction and for the maximum of achievement with the minimum of effort. In essence, we have ourselves created a drug-culture, in respect of which drugs in sport are simply one expression.[1]

Being founded on a holistic view of the body, in which exercise, diet and lifestyle factors are understood as parts of an interactive system, the Matrix principle extends this system approach to include psychological factors such as attitude and outlook, which are not seen as part of a separate 'mental realm' impermeable to the body but rather as extending and constantly interacting with it.

There is an increasing realisation today of the inter-relatedness of mind and body, and thus of the relevance of mental factors to health-related issues. The name of the seventeenth century French philosopher Descartes is (perhaps a trifle unfairly) linked to the notion of mind–body dualism, which was to be the prevailing view of human nature in Western society until modern times and still holds sway in many quarters. While Descartes did not invent this dualistic conception of the human person (often caricatured as 'a ghost driving a machine'), he certainly gave authoritative expression to an increasingly influential Western view which characterised the centuries of technological advance following his own age. As the twentieth century draws to a close, however, it is more and more common to hear a very different view put forward by scientists and medical practitioners. The physician Dr Larry Dossey MD, for example, has written:

> For over three hundred years Western civilisation has regarded all matter, including the body, as mindless. With the advent of modern science, however, the mind has come to be regarded as a special, sole property of the brain. Recently, this idea, too, has come under fire, as body tissues and organs distant from the brain have been discovered to possess brainlike

properties . . . In the wake of these developments, the old idea that the body is mindless seems increasingly illusory.[2]

Considerations such as these lay behind some of the experiments in bio-feedback which were conducted in the 1960s and extensively reported in the decade following. We have noted that some of the early promise of therapeutic benefit remained unfulfilled, although various biofeedback tech-niques have proved successful and confirmed the possibility of exploiting the mind–body connection for the treatment of certain illnesses.

PNI and the mind–body connection

More recent research has opened up even more fascinating possibilities in this general area. Beginning with some experiments by Robert Ader on Pavlovian conditioning in rats in the mid-1970s, this field has developed into a major research interest in universities world-wide, under the name of *psychoneuroimmunology* (PNI). In brief, Ader had been attempting to instil into the laboratory rats an aversion to saccharin-flavoured water: this he did by following the dose of sweet water with a drug (cyclophosphamide) which made the rats feel nauseous. As little as one dose of the drug was needed in order to establish an association on the animals' part with the sweet water. However, Ader noticed that a considerable number of the rats were beginning to die, and this could hardly be due to the saccharin. Other factors were also excluded. It was then that Ader realised what had happened: in addition to producing nausea, cyclophosphamide is a powerful immuno-suppressant (i.e. it suppresses the immune system which helps us resist disease). Now, the amount of the drug the rats had ingested was not sufficient to have this effect. But the association of the drug with saccharin was not only established in the rats' brains: it had also been established in their immune systems. So, whenever they drank the sweet water, their immune systems responded *as though* they had ingested cyclophos-phamide—and the result was premature death.[3]

Much experimental work followed, confirming Ader's findings. The term 'psychoneuroimmunology' was coined by him (on the basis of the existing term psychoimmunology) to give credit to the role of the central nervous system in the disease process. In 1981 there appeared the first edition of the massive volume *Psychoneuroimmunology*,[4] which brought together the work of experimental psychologists, psychiatrists, immunologists, neuro-anatomists, biologists and other scientists contributing to this discipline; a second edition in 1991 updated and added to the earlier research findings.

An important development took place in 1992 at the University of Newcastle, Australia, when a research team led by Professor M. G. King conducted a series of experiments on human beings. The researchers devel-oped a strange-tasting blue soft drink which the subjects drank at the same time as having a dust mite allergen or pollen placed up the nose. Afterwards, the subjects were given the blue drink on its own, without the allergen, yet

Athletes, such as top sprinter Trevor Lasky, are increasingly recognising the value of weight training.

a significant number had an allergic response, confirming Ader's results and extending them into new fields with enormous potential for the treatment of disease and illness.[5] Not the least exciting area of future development is that of transplant surgery: it is already known that when a guinea pig's immune system rejects a skin graft from a rabbit, and subsequently the guinea pig is given a local anaesthetic and a bandage applied to the site, the guinea pig's T cells will again display a rejection response even although this time there is nothing to reject.[6] If acceptance behaviour rather than rejection behaviour can be instilled by conditioning and association, the risks of transplant surgery may be considerably diminished.

At a less spectacular level, most people who have ever suffered from cold sores (the Type I herpes virus) will know that, once infected, they have the virus for life, and that after months or even years of lying dormant it may break out unpredictably. Among the factors believed to lead to an outbreak, stress seems always to play a major part, and it may well be that PNI research will lead to means of controlling the virus by techniques such as hypnotherapy. At a much more serious level of immune system attack, research at the University of California, San Francisco (UCSF), has for some years been attempting to apply PNI insights to the treatment of AIDS patients, with (to date) limited but promising results.[7]

Not a great deal of PNI research has focused directly on exercise, but the chapter by Harvey B. Simon ('Exercise and Human Immune Function') in *Psychoneuroimmunology*, Second Edition, indicates that both acute exercise and repetitive training produce complex changes in the tissues, cells and proteins of the immune system. The following passage is particularly relevant here:

Although the neuroendocrine effects of exercise mimic many aspects of the responses to psychic stress, there is evidence that endurance exercise actually relieves tension and produces relaxation and exhilaration. Improvements in mood, self-esteem, sexual function, and work behavior have been observed in healthy people who exercise and in patients undertaking exercise for cardiac rehabilitation. Acute exercise reduces anxiety and tension, but the response abates in 2 to 5 hours (Morgan, 1985). Habitual exercise has been associated with reduction in depression (Martinsen, Medhus, & Sandvik, 1985) and improved adaption to stress (Crews & Landers, 1987). Despite these preliminary findings, further quantitative studies are needed to determine if exercise is beneficial in treating some forms of anxiety and depression. In any case, although exercise-induced changes in monoamines and other neuropeptides, endorphins, and corticosteroids may importantly affect the immune system, it is less likely that the purely psychological effects of exercise exert important direct influences on human immune function.[8]

Some of the beneficial health outcomes of exercise (reduction of the risk of bowel cancer in men and of breast and reproductive tract cancer in women) are outside of Simon's purview as they are due to non-immuno-logical mechanisms. Those that he does mention include the release of endogenous pyrogen (also known as interleukin-1 or IL-1).[9] It has been suggested by Cannon and Kluger that this is part of an acute immune response which is a primitive protection mechanism arising from the days when people ran, not for exercise, but to escape danger: the production of IL-1 would thus be seen as a preparation for any injuries that might occur.[10] Simon's view is that 'these fascinating observations should be confirmed before we conclude that exercise hyperthermia involves the production of IL-1, much less immunologic enhancement'; and he points out that even when exercise does produce alterations in immune function, 'within minutes to hours after exercise ceases, most immune functions are back to normal'.[11] However, his conclusion leaves open the way for more positive future correlations in this area:

> We know that repeated exercise produces both short-term responses and long-term adaptation in the human systems, including cardiac and skeletal muscle, bone, and certain metabolic and endocrine functions. Further study will be required to learn if the transient immunologic responses to the stress of exercise can summate and result in biologically important phenomena.[12]

Some of these correlations between exercise and immune function have in fact begun to emerge in research appearing over the last few years. Lefavi and Deters have reported several recent studies of relevance to this area. They include findings which show that exercise significantly increases natural killer (NK) cell activity and thus improves resistance to infection; a study linking moderate-intensity exercise to the microbial activity of neutrophils, a similar disease-fighting response; and still other research indicating an exercise-induced increase in certain immunoglobins critical in combating micro-organisms and infection.[13] It is important to note that these studies relate to moderate exercise, whereas in the case of prolonged endurance exercise at high intensity there may well be an opposite effect: when the stress on the body becomes too high, the result may be a weakening of the immune system. Studies of marathon runners, for example, have shown decreased NK and T cell activity following a race (2–3 hours of running at marathon pace), indicating reduced resistance to disease until recuperation had taken place.

These findings are important in both their positive and their negative aspects. While supporting the proposition that exercise can have a beneficial effect on the immune function, they also underline the view that we have constantly reiterated in our presentation of the Matrix system—namely, that exercise, fitness and health are not synonymous terms. Exercise can in fact be stressful to the human organism—although most marathon runners are extremely fit individuals who recuperate rapidly from the immune-depressant effects of exhaustive exercise. Exercise itself is only one part of the larger complex of health-related factors, and it can work against the other factors if it passes a certain limit: below this limit stress elicits a positive adaptive response, whereas above this limit it becomes distress, the sign of inability to cope with the imposed load.

Among the other health-related factors is mental tension, which can be positive and creative but can also, like its physical counterpart, reach a level where it turns to stress or anxiety. A significant example of the connection between mind and body is the effect of exercise (although not over-exertion) in reducing mental and emotional stress. Locke and Colligan, for instance, cite the finding that muscle tension decreases in people after exercise and that the latter can act as a mild anxiety reducer and antidepressant; they add:

> To the PNI researcher the latter finding is significant, especially since depression is associated with a weakened immune system. Therefore, exercise is not only a natural antidepressant but, if psychoneuro-immunological evidence is correct, it may provide a kind of immunological insurance, especially for individuals susceptible to depression.[14]

Whether or not we accept the notion that the psychological effect of exercise may extend to enhancement of the immune function, the palpable effect of certain forms of exercise in promoting a feeling of mental ease and relaxation is beyond doubt. Research conducted during Matrix trials indicated that concentration on the rhythmic patterns on which Matrix exercise is built evoked in a significant number of participants a feeling of mental relaxation and well-being comparable to that derived from meditation techniques such as certain forms of yoga, and further research is currently in progress as to how this mind–body combination can be more effectively utilised as a therapeutic tool.

Adam Laura has been using Matrix training since childhood.

Positive health factors and the Matrix system

At a more general level, there is an increasing realisation among workers in this field that attention should be turned more to the enhancement of positive health factors, including positive emotions, rather than be concentrated almost exclusively on the treatment of symptoms arising from depressed mental and emotional states. Recent research by Dr David Phillips of the University of California, San Diego, would appear to confirm the need for such a change of emphasis. In a study of deaths among adult Chinese Americans and Caucasian (white) Americans dying in the same years and of the same diseases, Dr Phillips's team found that Chinese Americans who had a combination of disease and birth-year believed by them to be ill-fated, actually died earlier than white Americans who did not share their beliefs. This research, published in *The Lancet*, was based on the analysis of some 440 000 records, and the researchers were careful to examine possible alternative explanations (e.g. a change to an unhealthy lifestyle in the belief that death was inevitable) before excluding them. The authors of the study concluded: ' . . . Our findings result at least partly from psychosomatic processes. More broadly, our data suggest that psychosomatic factors can profoundly affect the longevity of patients with most diseases'.[15]

The Matrix system is directed at playing a small part in the contemporary movement towards fostering positive mental and emotional states, using the established correlation between exercise and improved self-image, tension reduction and mood enhancement as one of its main bases. Along with other, more obvious correlations such as the exercise–health connection and the link between nutritionally-appropriate natural food and overall well-being, the positive psychological outcomes of exercise are not only of value for their own sake, but can also reinforce the physical training effect through the influence of our psychological state on our overall health. As one of the most distinguished of PNI researchers, David L. Felten, has written:

> We are beginning to document how some stressors and some distressing events and affective states such as depression and bereavement may be associated with adverse health outcomes and diminished measures of immune response under some circumstances; unfortunately, little attention has been given to the scientific examination of the counterpart, namely, that positive emotions may contribute to beneficial health outcomes and enhanced immune responsiveness.[16]

The increasing interest of the medical and scientific communities in the mind–body connection and the influence of attitudinal and emotional factors on physical health does not always receive an amount of public exposure commensurate with the truly fundamental turnaround that it represents in medical practice.

This change in attitude is observable in areas such as the information given to patients. The practice of doctors not telling seriously ill patients what is wrong with them is of long standing; it may even go back as far as Hippocrates, who taught that it is better for patients not to know the nature of their illness, as distracting them from it was part of their treatment. Whatever its origins, the mechanistic Western view of the human organism derived from the Cartesian dualism of mind and body fitted in well with the ancient teaching. The understanding of the body as an object separate from our selves led to a 'code of silence' in Western medicine which is only now being abandoned in the teaching of patient care. A growing number of doctors and medical educators in Western societies are adopting the view that patients should be informed of their medical condition not merely as a matter of ethics but also in order that the whole person, mind and body, can be cared for as an entity – not just as a medical case or an assemblage of symptoms, but as a person whose state of mind may both need as much therapeutic care as their physical condition and may indeed influence that condition significantly.

Not only among doctors, but also among their patients, attitudes towards the mind–body relationship are moving away from the traditional narrow compartmentalisation. A survey published in 1994 in the *Medical Journal of Australia* on children undergoing cancer treatment revealed that some 46% of these patients had used at least one alternative therapy, usually in addition to orthodox treatments such as chemotherapy. Of these complementary therapies, the most common was positive imagery (17%), followed by hypnotherapy and mental imagery (15% each) and relaxation exercises

(10%). The study, conducted by proponents of orthodox medical treatment, was concerned not so much with the question of whether complementary therapies are effective, as with the fact they fill a gap not being met by conventional medical treatment.[17] Indeed, it would be surprising if at least some of these therapies were without positive results, even if only as a consequence of the so-called 'placebo effect'. Repeated clinical trials have revealed positive responses to a medicine or treatment which cannot be attributed to its chemical or physical properties: the average proportion of people who respond positively to a placebo (or dummy treatment) is 33%, and can be as high as 95% for some conditions. The placebo effect has been shown to cause physical changes such as reducing blood pressure, healing ulcers and reducing facial swelling. A placebo can even overrule the normal effect of a drug: volunteers given amphetamines (stimulants), but told they are sedatives, become sedated.[18] All in all, there is strong and growing evidence that mental attitude and belief can have powerful physical consequences: even the orthodox medical profession is increasingly accepting and actively using mental processes as therapeutic strategies.

Along with this revision in medical attitudes has come a new interest on the part of many weight trainers, athletes and sportspersons generally in the use of their exercise regime for stress reduction, relaxation therapy and other 'spin-off' effects aimed at mental well-being as much as the purely physical training outcomes. New technologies, based on a holistic approach to the mind–body complex, are being recruited into the workout, and such devices as light and sound (LS) machines, acoustic field systems, and sophisticated audiotapes are becoming more and more common in fitness centres.[19] In addition, bodybuilding magazines are increasingly running series of articles on positive adjuncts to weight training: meditation, yoga, acupuncture and acupressure, and a variety of 'alternative' or non-traditional therapies are again finding a place in serious writing on sports and fitness, as they are in parts of the medical and scientific literature.

For too long, bodybuilders and even some elite athletes have tended to treat their bodies as objects somehow removed from their 'real' selves. The body could be subjected to rigorous training, punished or stressed beyond its natural limits, or pumped full of performance-enhancing drugs, and still be expected not to rebel against such treatment. The body all too often managed to take its revenge in terms of injury, breakdown and (in the case of drug use) serious illness and even death. The newer consciousness of the human person as a single, indivisible entity of body, mind and spirit is radically changing the face of sports training and physical exercise generally: the latter is coming to be seen as mental therapy as much as a physical maintenance program, and all sorts of social groupings from business executives and working mothers to retirees and psychiatric patients are coming to appreciate the interconnectedness of physical well-being, emotional health and relief of stress-related symptoms.

In the series of books making up the Matrix trilogy, we have attempted to cater for the needs of all those wishing to enter or make progress in the world of physical training, from raw beginners to elite athletes and bodybuilders. While the exercise routines move from the relatively simple and easy to the more complex and demanding, the system of which they are a part applies with equal relevance to all trainers regardless of age, sex, stage of training or ultimate training goal. The authors hope that the examples quoted in the course of the above discussion will serve to under-line the extent to which the control over our bodies that we can derive from Matrix training can influence the control we can take over many other aspects of our lives. And from that feeling of being in control, rather than being controlled, should arise an enormous sense of freedom and an enhanced enjoyment of the experience of living.

Part 2

The ultimate Matrix workout program

Anthony Wingett shows the quality muscle that has won him numerous bodybuilding titles including Mr Universe.

5 The Advanced Matrix techniques

In this final volume of the Matrix system trilogy, the focus will be on the last twelve of the 36 Matrix techniques, which are presented here for the first time.

You will find a complete list of the 36 core Matrix techniques in the appendix. The techniques numbered 25 to 36 on the list are those on which the training schedules in this book are based: they make up the Ultimate Workout regime which is the culmination of the training method introduced in our earlier works *The Matrix Principle* (techniques 1–12) and *Matrix for Muscle Gain* (techniques 12–24).

In order to save space, we have not set out the twelve-month Ultimate Workout regime in total detail, indicating every repetition of every exercise for each day of the year. Not only would this have added inordinately to the length of this book and made it unwieldy to use, but it would probably have been unnecessary since almost all users of the Ultimate Workout system will already be experienced Matrix trainers who are by now familiar with how Matrix exercise proceeds and how the various repetition patterns are applied from one exercise to another.

The idea, then, is that each trainer constructs his or her own weekly schedule according to the principles outlined below. It is simply a matter of understanding the *principles* on which the twelve-month training period is built, and then applying them from one week to another throughout the year.

What are these principles? As with so much in the world of Matrix training, they may at first look a little complicated, but once you have taken the trouble to see how they are built up, and the rational pattern lying behind them, you will see how easy they are to follow.

The first principle is that each exercise in the workout is made up of *four sets*, each of them using a different Matrix technique. (As stated above, the techniques used in this book are those numbered from 25 to 36 in the complete Matrix system—in other words, they are the final twelve, or Advanced, techniques.)

The four techniques (one for each set) are used in numerical order—for example, 25, 26, 27 and 28. If you look at the complete list of Matrix techniques in the appendix, you will see that these are as follows:

- 25 is the Single Iso-Matrix Triad;
- 26 is the Double Iso-Matrix Triad;
- 27 is the Triple Iso-Matrix Triad; and
- 28 is the Single Mixed Matrix.

These are the four techniques used for Month 1. This means that, in the first month of your Ultimate Workout regime, *every exercise* that you do consists of *four sets*, one of each technique. The first set will be the Single Iso-Matrix Triad, the second set will be the Double Iso-Matrix Triad, and so on.

When you have completed the first month's training, you move on to Month 2. This is constructed in exactly the same way as Month 1, except that in this month the techniques are not those numbered 25 to 28, but those numbered 26 to 29. In other words, you move further down the list of Matrix techniques each month, introducing a new technique and leaving out a technique which has already been used (generally for four months).

Table 5.1 shows how your year's training is constructed on this rotational basis, and should clarify the above explanation if it is not already clear. To help you become accustomed to how the Ultimate Workout program is constructed, the first month's routines are set out in full in chapters 6 to 11. By the end of this first month, you should be sufficiently familiar with the system to be able to follow its basic principles (i.e. its rotational basis) for the other eleven months, without the need for each individual body part routine to be shown in detail. In other words, you will work the same body parts on the same days as in Month 1—but using a slightly different group of techniques each month.

Our Matrix clinics have shown that one month is an adequate time for trainers to learn the various patterns involved, but not enough time for their bodies to adjust completely to the continuously varying training intensity required. The muscles are thus continuously 'shocked' into new adaptations as the workouts push the trainer to the limit in virtually every exercise, and certainly by the completion of each four-set sequence.

Another important principle is that of *increasing intensity*. Experienced Matrix trainers are already aware that this form of high-intensity training aims at maintaining short pauses between sets: the goal is to reduce the pauses from the conventional minute or two (or longer), down to the times specified in the Matrix program (often 15 seconds, although in some cases slightly more or less than this).

In the Ultimate Workout program, the same general principle applies, with the added proviso that there are *three stages* (known as Advanced Stages I, II and III) through which trainers move as their proficiency increases. These are set out in Tables 5.2 to 5.4.

Table 5.1   The Ultimate workout program

Month	1	2	3	4	5	6	7	8	9	10	11	12	
Set 1	25 Single Iso-Matrix Triad	26 Double Iso-Matrix Triad	27 Triple Iso-Matrix Triad	28 Single Mixed Matrix	29 Double Mixed Matrix	30 Triple Mixed Matrix	31 Single Mixed Iso-Matrix	32 Double Mixed Iso-Matrix	33 Triple Mixed Iso-Matrix	34 Cumulative Iso-Matrix Reversals	35 Iso-Matrix Alternates	36 Mixed Matrix Composites	Set 1
Set 2	26 Double Iso-Matrix Triad	27 Triple Iso-Matrix Triad	28 Single Mixed Matrix	29 Double Mixed Matrix	30 Triple Mixed Matrix	31 Single Mixed Iso-Matrix	32 Double Mixed Iso-Matrix	33 Triple Mixed Iso-Matrix	34 Cumulative Iso-Matrix Reversals	35 Iso-Matrix Alternates	36 Mixed Matrix Composites	25 Single Iso-Matrix Triad	Set 2
Set 3	27 Triple Iso-Matrix Triad	28 Single Mixed Matrix	29 Double Mixed Matrix	30 Triple Mixed Matrix	31 Single Mixed Iso-Matrix	32 Double Mixed Iso-Matrix	33 Triple Mixed Iso-Matrix	34 Cumulative Iso-Matrix Reversals	35 Iso-Matrix Alternates	36 Mixed Matrix Composites	25 Single Iso-Matrix Triad	26 Double Iso-Matrix Triad	Set 3
Set 4	28 Single Mixed Matrix	29 Double Mixed Matrix	30 Triple Mixed Matrix	31 Single Mixed Iso-Matrix	32 Double Mixed Iso-Matrix	33 Triple Mixed Iso-Matrix	34 Cumulative Iso-Matrix Reversals	35 Iso-Matrix Alternates	36 Mixed Matrix Composites	25 Single Iso-Matrix Triad	26 Double Iso-Matrix Triad	27 Triple Iso-Matrix Triad	Set 4

Table 5.2   Advanced Stage I

Mon.	Tues.	Wed.	Thur.	Fri.	Sat.	Sun.
Chest	Biceps	Thighs	Upper back	Biceps	Chest	Rest day
Shoulders	Triceps	Calves	Lower back	Triceps	Shoulders	
Abdominals	Forearms	Abdominals		Forearms	Abdominals	
				Calves		

Notice that on this schedule every body part is worked at least twice per week, with the exception of the thighs and the upper and lower back. The assumption here is that by the time you reach the advanced training program, one intensive Matrix back or upper leg session per week will be sufficient. If you feel that your back or upper leg needs to be trained more than once per week, two options are available:

1. substitute the back or thigh routine for some other body part routine—for example, you could replace your Friday calf workout with the back or thigh routine; or
2. add your back or thigh routine to any other workout session you choose, as long as you give yourself one day's rest between the back or thigh-training sessions.

Progression through the stages is as follows. Once you are able to complete Advanced Stage I *in accordance with the specified pause periods between sets*, you are ready to move to the next stage. How long you remain at Stage I or Stage II will thus depend on your level of fitness. We strongly recommend that you do not try to 'cheat'; rather, you should ensure that you do not move to the next stage until you are able to perform the routines at the lower stage *at the level of intensity indicated*.

The above instructions presuppose that, at first, you will not be able to complete the routines with the pauses specified: this is perfectly normal, since your goal is to *improve* your ability over a period of time. You may need at first to pause for longer than the allotted period, but as you progress your goal should be to reduce the rest periods to those set out in the program. Similarly, you may need to give yourself more recuperation time by pausing briefly within the set itself. If you are unable to complete the repetition pattern within a single set, simply put the weight down for a break of, say, 10 or 20 seconds before resuming where you left off. Continue this pattern of breaks until you can finish the set. Once again, your goal should be to complete each set without internal breaks.

If you find, on beginning Advanced Stage I, that the workout (with the pauses as indicated) is too easy to complete, increase the weight by jumps of 5 kg until the load is satisfactory. Conversely, if the sequence is so difficult that you cannot complete it or need extra-long pauses, you are probably using too much weight and should try decreasing it by 5 kg until

Table 5.3   Advanced Stage II

Mon.	Tues.	Wed.	Thur.	Fri.	Sat.	Sun. (optional)
Thighs	Biceps	Chest	Thighs	Chest	Thighs	Chest
Lower back	Triceps	Forearms	Lower back	Biceps	Shoulders	Upper back
Upper back	Shoulders	Calves	Upper back	Triceps	Calves	Abdominals
Abdominals	Abdominals		Abdominals	Forearms	Abdominals	
Calves						

Table 5.4   Advanced Stage III

Mon.	Tues.	Wed.	Thur.	Fri.	Sat.	Sun. (optional)
Chest	Lower back	Chest	Thighs	Upper back	Chest	Upper back
Thighs	Upper back	Biceps	Calves	Lower back	Thighs	Lower back
Calves					Calves	
Biceps	Shoulders	Triceps	Abdominals	Shoulders	Biceps	
Triceps	Abdominals	Forearms			Triceps	
Forearms		Abdominals			Forearms	

the load is satisfactory and the routine can be completed with a high degree of challenge to the muscles, but without complete muscle failure.

It cannot be stressed too strongly that *proper form* needs to be maintained with each movement. Incorrect form increases the risk of injury, as well as reducing the growth-enhancing effect of Matrix-style exercise. If you are using sloppy form, you can often shift a greater weight, but because the target muscles are not fully isolated much of the effort is dissipated and ineffective.

6 Monday training routine (month 1): chest, shoulders and abdominals

Chest

Exercise A: Pec Deck

(Tick the box when you've completed the relevant exercise.)

Set 1:   *Single Iso-Matrix Triad*
5 full reps
+
3 reps half-up
3 reps half-down
+
1 rep half-up (holding in the half position for 3 seconds)
1 rep half-down (holding in the half position for 3 seconds)
+
5 full reps
☐

15 seconds pause between sets

Set 2:   *Double Iso-Matrix Triad*
5 full reps
+
3 reps half-up
3 reps half-down
+
2 reps half-up (holding in the half position for 3 seconds)
2 reps half-down (holding in the half position for 3 seconds)
+
5 full reps
☐

15 seconds pause between sets

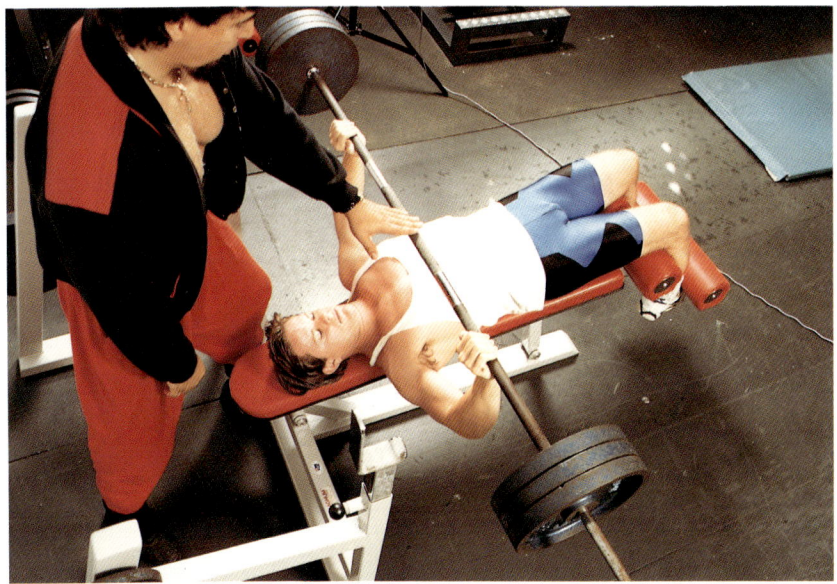

Bench Press with Barbell

Set 3: *Triple Iso-Matrix Triad*
   5 full reps
      +
   3 reps half-up
   3 reps half-down
      +
   3 reps half-up (holding in the half position for 3 seconds)
   3 reps half-down (holding in the half position for 3 seconds)
      +
   5 full reps

☐

   20 seconds pause between sets

Set 4: *Single Mixed Matrix*
   5 full reps
      +
   1 rep one-fifth up
   1 rep half-up
      +
   1 rep one-fifth down
   1 rep half-down
      +
   5 full reps

☐

   Rest 1 minute between exercises

Exercise B: Bench Press with Barbell (vary the position of hands with each set)

(Tick the box when you've completed the relevant exercise.)

Set 1: *Single Iso-Matrix Triad*
5 full reps
+
3 reps half-up
3 reps half-down
+
1 rep half-up (holding in the half position for 3 seconds)
1 rep half-down (holding in the half position for 3 seconds)
+
5 full reps

☐

15 seconds pause between sets

Set 2: *Double Iso-Matrix Triad*
5 full reps
+
3 reps half-up
3 reps half-down
+
2 reps half-up (holding in the half position for 3 seconds)
2 reps half-down (holding in the half position for 3 seconds)
+
5 full reps

☐

15 seconds pause between sets

Set 3: *Triple Iso-Matrix Triad*
5 full reps
+
3 reps half-up
3 reps half-down
+
3 reps half-up (holding in the half position for 3 seconds)
3 reps half-down (holding in the half position for 3 seconds)
+
5 full reps

☐

20 seconds pause between sets

Set 4: *Single Mixed Matrix*
      5 full reps
        +
      1 rep one-fifth up
      1 rep half-up
        +
      1 rep one-fifth down
      1 rep half-down
        +
      5 full reps

      ☐

Rest one minute between exercises

Exercise C: Incline Bench Press with Dumbbells

(Tick the box when you've completed the relevant exercise.)

Set 1: *Single Iso-Matrix Triad*
      5 full reps
        +
      3 reps half-up
      3 reps half-down
        +
      1 rep half-up (holding in the half position for 3 seconds)
      1 rep half-down (holding in the half position for 3 seconds)
        +
      5 full reps

      ☐

15 seconds pause between sets

Set 2: *Double Iso-Matrix Triad*
      5 full reps
        +
      3 reps half-up
      3 reps half-down
        +
      2 reps half-up (holding in the half position for 3 seconds)
      2 reps half-down (holding in the half position for 3 seconds)
        +
      5 full reps

      ☐

15 seconds pause between sets

Set 3: *Triple Iso-Matrix Triad*
    5 full reps
       +
    3 reps half-up
    3 reps half-down
       +
    3 reps half-up (holding in the half position for 3 seconds)
    3 reps half-down (holding in the half position for 3 seconds)
       +
    5 full reps

    20 seconds pause between sets

Set 4: *Single Mixed Matrix*
    5 full reps
       +
    1 rep one-fifth up
    1 rep half-up
       +
    1 rep one-fifth down
    1 rep half-down
       +
    5 full reps

Rest 3 minutes before proceeding to the next body part exercise

Shoulders

Exercise A: Matrix Roll Press

Note: Half-position to be executed behind the neck for the first set, in front of neck for the second set, behind the neck for the third set and in front for the fourth set.
(Tick the box when you've completed the relevant exercise.)

Set 1: *Single Iso-Matrix Triad*
　　　5 Matrix Roll reps
　　　　+
　　　3 reps half-up
　　　3 reps half-down
　　　　+
　　　1 rep half-up (holding in the half position for 3 seconds)
　　　1 rep half-down (holding in the half position for 3 seconds)
　　　　+
　　　5 Matrix Roll reps □

　　　15 seconds pause between sets

Set 2: *Double Iso-Matrix Triad*
　　　5 Matrix Roll reps
　　　　+
　　　3 reps half-up
　　　3 reps half-down
　　　　+
　　　2 reps half-up (holding in the half position for 3 seconds)
　　　2 reps half-down (holding in the half position for 3 seconds)
　　　　+
　　　5 Matrix Roll reps □

　　　15 seconds pause between sets

Set 3: *Triple Iso-Matrix Triad*
　　　5 Matrix Roll reps
　　　　+
　　　3 reps half-up
　　　3 reps half-down
　　　　+
　　　3 reps half-up (holding in the half position for 3 seconds)
　　　3 reps half-down (holding in the half position for 3 seconds)
　　　　+
　　　5 Matrix Roll reps □

　　　20 seconds pause between sets

Set 4: *Single Mixed Matrix*
   5 Matrix Roll reps
      +
   1 rep one-fifth up
   1 rep half-up
      +
   1 rep one-fifth down
   1 rep half-down
      +
   5 Matrix Roll reps

□

Rest 1 minute between exercises

Exercise B: Lateral Raises with Dumbbells (vary the position of hands with each set)

(Tick the box when you've completed the relevant exercise.)

Set 1: *Single Iso-Matrix Triad*
   5 full reps
      +
   3 reps half-up
   3 reps half-down
      +
   1 rep half-up (holding in the half position for 3 seconds)
   1 rep half-down (holding in the half position for 3 seconds)
      +
   5 full reps

□

15 seconds pause between sets

Set 2: *Double Iso-Matrix Triad*
   5 full reps
      +
   3 reps half-up
   3 reps half-down
      +
   2 reps half-up (holding in the half position for 3 seconds)
   2 reps half-down (holding in the half position for 3 seconds)
      +
   5 full reps

□

15 seconds pause between sets

Set 3: *Triple Iso-Matrix Triad*
      5 full reps
       +
      3 reps half-up
      3 reps half-down
       +
      3 reps half-up (holding in the half position for 3 seconds)
      3 reps half-down (holding in the half position for 3 seconds)
       +
      5 full reps

      ☐

20 seconds pause between sets

Set 4: *Single Mixed Matrix*
      5 full reps
       +
      1 rep one-fifth up
      1 rep half-up
       +
      1 rep one-fifth down
      1 rep half-down
       +
      5 full reps

      ☐

Rest 1 minute between exercises

Exercise C: Dumbbell Front Raises

(Tick the box when you've completed the relevant exercise.)

Set 1: *Single Iso-Matrix Triad*
      5 full reps
       +
      3 reps half-up
      3 reps half-down
       +
      1 rep half-up (holding in the half position for 3 seconds)
      1 rep half-down (holding in the half position for 3 seconds)
       +
      5 full reps

      ☐

15 seconds pause between sets

Lateral Raises with Dumbbells (starting position)

Set 2: *Double Iso-Matrix Triad*
   5 full reps
      +
   3 reps half-up
   3 reps half-down
      +
   2 reps half-up (holding in the half position for 3 seconds)
   2 reps half-down (holding in the half position for 3 seconds)
      +
   5 full reps

   15 seconds pause between sets

Set 3: *Triple Iso-Matrix Triad*
   5 full reps
      +
   3 reps half-up
   3 reps half-down
      +
   3 reps half-up (holding in the half position for 3 seconds)
   3 reps half-down (holding in the half position for 3 seconds)
      +
   5 full reps

   20 seconds pause between sets

Set 4: *Single Mixed Matrix*
        5 full reps
            +
        1 rep one-fifth up
        1 rep half-up
            +
        1 rep one-fifth down
        1 rep half-down
            +
        5 full reps

☐

Rest 3 minutes before proceeding to the next body part exercise

Abdominals

Exercise A: Flat Bench Leg Raises

(Tick the box when you've completed the relevant exercise.)

Set 1: *Single Iso-Matrix Triad*
        5 full reps
            +
        3 reps half-up
        3 reps half-down
            +
        1 rep half-up (holding in the half position for 3 seconds)
        1 rep half-down (holding in the half position for 3 seconds)
            +
        5 full reps

☐

15 seconds pause between sets

Set 2: *Double Iso-Matrix Triad*
        5 full reps
            +
        3 reps half-up
        3 reps half-down
            +
        2 reps half-up (holding in the half position for 3 seconds)
        2 reps half-down (holding in the half position for 3 seconds)
            +
        5 full reps

☐

15 seconds pause between sets

Set 3: *Triple Iso-Matrix Triad*
　　　　5 full reps
　　　　　　+
　　　　3 reps half-up
　　　　3 reps half-down
　　　　　　+
　　　　3 reps half-up (holding in the half position for 3 seconds)
　　　　3 reps half-down (holding in the half position for 3 seconds)
　　　　　　+
　　　　5 full reps

□

　　　　20 seconds pause between sets

Set 4: *Single Mixed Matrix*
　　　　5 full reps
　　　　　　+
　　　　1 rep one-fifth up
　　　　1 rep half-up
　　　　　　+
　　　　1 rep one-fifth down
　　　　1 rep half-down
　　　　　　+
　　　　5 full reps

□

　　　　Rest one minute between exercises

Exercise B: Incline Board Sit-ups

(Tick the box when you've completed the relevant exercise).

Set 1: *Single Iso-Matrix Triad*
　　　　5 full reps
　　　　　　+
　　　　3 reps half-up
　　　　3 reps half-down
　　　　　　+
　　　　1 rep half-up (holding in the half position for 3 seconds)
　　　　1 rep half-down (holding in the half position for 3 seconds)
　　　　　　+
　　　　5 full reps

□

　　　　15 seconds pause between sets

An alternative exercise for the abs and obliques.

Set 2: *Double Iso-Matrix Triad*
      5 full reps
        +
      3 reps half-up
      3 reps half-down
        +
      2 reps half-up (holding in the half position for 3 seconds)
      2 reps half-down (holding in the half position for 3 seconds)
        +
      5 full reps

      15 seconds pause between sets

Set 3: *Triple Iso-Matrix Triad*
      5 full reps
        +
      3 reps half-up
      3 reps half-down
        +
      3 reps half-up (holding in the half position for 3 seconds)
      3 reps half-down (holding in the half position for 3 seconds)
        +
      5 full reps

      20 seconds pause between sets

Set 4: *Single Mixed Matrix*
   5 full reps

   +

   1 rep one-fifth up
   1 rep half-up

   +

   1 rep one-fifth down
   1 rep half-down

   +

   5 full reps

Rest 1 minute between exercises

Exercise C: High Chair Leg Raises

(Tick the box when you've completed the relevant exercise.)

Set 1: *Single Iso-Matrix Triad*
   5 full reps

   +

   3 reps half-up
   3 reps half-down

   +

   1 rep half-up (holding in the half position for 3 seconds)
   1 rep half-down (holding in the half position for 3 seconds)

   +

   5 full reps

15 seconds pause between sets

Set 2: *Double Iso-Matrix Triad*
   5 full reps

   +

   3 reps half-up
   3 reps half-down

   +

   2 reps half-up (holding in the half position for 3 seconds)
   2 reps half-down (holding in the half position for 3 seconds)

   +

   5 full reps

15 seconds pause between sets

Set 3: *Triple Iso-Matrix Triad*
        5 full reps
          +
        3 reps half-up
        3 reps half-down
          +
        3 reps half-up (holding in the half position for 3 seconds)
        3 reps half-down (holding in the half position for 3 seconds)
          +
        5 full reps

☐

20 seconds pause between sets

Set 4: *Single Mixed Matrix*
        5 full reps
          +
        1 rep one-fifth up
        1 rep half-up
          +
        1 rep one-fifth down
        1 rep half-down
          +
        5 full reps

☐

Finish of Monday training routine

7 Tuesday training routine (month 1): biceps, triceps and forearms

Biceps

Exercise A: Preacher Bench Curls with EZ Curl Bar

(Tick the box when you've completed the relevant exercise.

Set 1: *Single Iso-Matrix Triad*
5 full reps
   +
3 reps one-half up
3 reps one-half down
   +
1 rep one-half up (holding in the half position for 3 seconds)
1 rep one-half down (holding in the half position for 3 seconds)
   +
5 full reps

☐

15 seconds pause between sets

Set 2: *Double Iso-Matrix Triad*
5 full reps
   +
3 reps one-half up
3 reps one-half down
   +
2 reps one-half up (holding in the half position for 3 seconds)
2 reps one-half down (holding in the half position for 3 seconds)
   +
5 full reps

☐

15 seconds pause between sets

The remarkable forearm development of Adam Laura.

Set 3: *Triple Iso-Matrix Triad*
5 full reps
+
3 reps one-half up
3 reps one-half down
+
3 reps one-half up (holding in the half position for 3 seconds)
3 reps one-half down (holding in the half position for 3 seconds)
+
5 full reps

20 seconds pause between sets

Set 4: *Single Mixed Matrix*
5 full reps
+
1 rep one-fifth up
1 rep one-half up
+
1 rep one-fifth down
1 rep one-half down
+
5 full reps

Rest 1 minute between exercises

Exercise B: Incline Bench Dumbbell Curls

(Tick the box when you've completed the relevant exercise.)

Set 1: *Single Iso-Matrix Triad*
   5 full reps
    +
   3 reps one-half up
   3 reps one-half down
    +
   1 rep one-half up (holding in the half position for 3 seconds)
   1 rep one-half down (holding in the half position for 3 seconds)
    +
   5 full reps

☐

   15 seconds pause between sets

Set 2: *Double Iso-Matrix Triad*
   5 full reps
    +
   3 reps one-half up
   3 reps one-half down
    +
   2 reps one-half up (holding in the half position for 3 seconds)
   2 reps one-half down (holding in the half position for 3 seconds)
    +
   5 full reps

☐

   15 seconds pause between sets

Set 3: *Triple Iso-Matrix Triad*
   5 full reps
    +
   3 reps one-half up
   3 reps one-half down
    +
   3 reps one-half up (holding in the half position for 3 seconds)
   3 reps one-half down (holding in the half position for 3 seconds)
    +
   5 full reps

☐

   20 seconds pause between sets

Set 4: *Single Mixed Matrix*
        5 full reps
          +
        1 rep one-fifth up
        1 rep one-half up
          +
        1 rep one-fifth down
        1 rep one-half down
          +
        5 full reps

☐

Rest 1 minute between exercises

Exercise C: Standing Barbell Curls

(Tick the box when you've completed the relevant exercise.)

Set 1: *Single Iso-Matrix Triad*
        5 full reps
          +
        3 reps one-half up
        3 reps one-half down
          +
        1 rep one-half up (holding in the half position for 3 seconds)
        1 rep one-half down (holding in the half position for 3 seconds)
          +
        5 full reps

☐

15 seconds pause between sets

Set 2: *Double Iso-Matrix Triad*
        5 full reps
          +
        3 reps one-half up
        3 reps one-half down
          +
        2 reps one-half up (holding in the half position for 3 seconds)
        2 reps one-half down (holding in the half position for 3 seconds)
          +
        5 full reps

☐

15 seconds pause between sets

Standing Barbell Curls

Set 3: *Triple Iso-Matrix Triad*
   5 full reps
      +
   3 reps one-half up
   3 reps one-half down
      +
   3 reps one-half up (holding in the half position for 3 seconds)
   3 reps one-half down (holding in the half position for 3 seconds)
      +
   5 full reps

☐

   20 seconds pause between sets

Set 4: *Single Mixed Matrix*
   5 full reps
      +
   1 rep one-fifth up
   1 rep one-half up
      +
   1 rep one-fifth down
   1 rep one-half down
      +
   5 full reps

☐

   Rest 3 minutes before proceeding to the next body part exercise

Triceps Pushdowns

Triceps

Exercise A: Triceps Pushdowns

(Tick the box when you've completed the relevant exercise.)

Set 1: *Single Iso-Matrix Triad*
       5 full reps
         +
       3 reps one-half up
       3 reps one-half down
         +
       1 rep one-half up (holding in the half position for 3 seconds)
       1 rep one-half down (holding in the half position for 3 seconds)
         +
       5 full reps

       ☐

       15 seconds pause between sets

Set 2: *Double Iso-Matrix Triad*
 5 full reps
  +
 3 reps one-half up
 3 reps one-half down
  +
 2 reps one-half up (holding in the half position for 3 seconds)
 2 reps one-half down (holding in the half position for 3 seconds)
  +
 5 full reps

☐

 15 seconds pause between sets

Set 3: *Triple Iso-Matrix Triad*
 5 full reps
  +
 3 reps one-half up
 3 reps one-half down
  +
 3 reps one-half up (holding in the half position for 3 seconds)
 3 reps one-half down (holding in the half position for 3 seconds)
  +
 5 full reps

☐

 20 seconds pause between sets

Set 4: *Single Mixed Matrix*
 5 full reps
  +
 1 rep one-fifth up
 1 rep one-half up
  +
 1 rep one-fifth down
 1 rep one-half down
  +
 5 full reps

☐

 Rest 1 minute between exercises

Exercise B: Standing Triceps Press with Dumbbell

(Tick the box when you've completed the relevant exercise.)

Set 1: *Single Iso-Matrix Triad*
        5 full reps
            +
        3 reps one-half up
        3 reps one-half down
            +
        1 rep one-half up (holding in the half position for 3 seconds)
        1 rep one-half down (holding in the half position for 3 seconds)
            +
        5 full reps

                                                                        ☐

        15 seconds pause between sets

Set 2: *Double Iso-Matrix Triad*
        5 full reps
            +
        3 reps one-half up
        3 reps one-half down
            +
        2 reps one-half up (holding in the half position for 3 seconds)
        2 reps one-half down (holding in the half position for 3 seconds)
            +
        5 full reps

                                                                        ☐

        15 seconds pause between sets

Set 3: *Triple Iso-Matrix Triad*
        5 full reps
            +
        3 reps one-half up
        3 reps one-half down
            +
        3 reps one-half up (holding in the half position for 3 seconds)
        3 reps one-half down (holding in the half position for 3 seconds)
            +
        5 full reps

                                                                        ☐

        20 seconds pause between sets

Set 4: *Single Mixed Matrix*
        5 full reps
            +
        1 rep one-fifth up
        1 rep one-half up
            +
        1 rep one-fifth down
        1 rep one-half down
            +
        5 full reps

        ☐

        Rest 1 minute between exercises

Exercise C: Lying Triceps Press with EZ Curl Bar

(Tick the box when you've completed the relevant exercise.)

Set 1: *Single Iso-Matrix Triad*
        5 full reps
            +
        3 reps one-half up
        3 reps one-half down
            +
        1 rep one-half up (holding in the half position for 3 seconds)
        1 rep one-half down (holding in the half position for 3 seconds)
            +
        5 full reps

        ☐

        15 seconds pause between sets

Set 2: *Double Iso-Matrix Triad*
        5 full reps
            +
        3 reps one-half up
        3 reps one-half down
            +
        2 reps one-half up (holding in the half position for 3 seconds)
        2 reps one-half down (holding in the half position for 3 seconds)
            +
        5 full reps

        ☐

        15 seconds pause between sets

Set 3: *Triple Iso-Matrix Triad*
    5 full reps
      +
    3 reps one-half up
    3 reps one-half down
      +
    3 reps one-half up (holding in the half position for 3 seconds)
    3 reps one-half down (holding in the half position for 3 seconds)
      +
    5 full reps

☐

20 seconds pause between sets

Set 4: *Single Mixed Matrix*
    5 full reps
      +
    1 rep one-fifth up
    1 rep one-half up
      +
    1 rep one-fifth down
    1 rep one-half down
      +
    5 full reps

☐

Rest 3 minutes before proceeding to the next body part exercise

Forearms

Exercise A: Seated Wrist Curl with Barbell

(Tick the box when you've completed the relevant exercise.)

Set 1: *Single Iso-Matrix Triad*
    5 full reps
      +
    3 reps one-half up
    3 reps one-half down
      +
    1 rep one-half up (holding in the half position for 3 seconds)
    1 rep one-half down (holding in the half position for 3 seconds)
      +
    5 full reps

☐

15 seconds pause between sets

Set 2: *Double Iso-Matrix Triad*
        5 full reps
            +
        3 reps one-half up
        3 reps one-half down
            +
        2 reps one-half up (holding in the half position for 3 seconds)
        2 reps one-half down (holding in the half position for 3 seconds)
            +
        5 full reps

☐

15 seconds pause between sets

Set 3: *Triple Iso-Matrix Triad*
        5 full reps
            +
        3 reps one-half up
        3 reps one-half down
            +
        3 reps one-half up (holding in the half position for 3 seconds)
        3 reps one-half down (holding in the half position for 3 seconds)
            +
        5 full reps

☐

20 seconds pause between sets

Set 4: *Single Mixed Matrix*
        5 full reps
            +
        1 rep one-fifth up
        1 rep one-half up
            +
        1 rep one-fifth down
        1 rep one-half down
            +
        5 full reps

☐

Rest 1 minute between exercises

Seated Wrist Curl with Barbell

Exercise B: Seated Reverse Wrist Curl with Dumbbells

(Tick the box when you've completed the relevant exercise.)

Set 1: *Single Iso-Matrix Triad*
    5 full reps
      +
    3 reps one-half up
    3 reps one-half down
      +
    1 rep one-half up (holding in the half position for 3 seconds)
    1 rep one-half down (holding in the half position for 3 seconds)
      +
    5 full reps

15 seconds pause between sets

Set 2: *Double Iso-Matrix Triad*
          5 full reps
              +
          3 reps one-half up
          3 reps one-half down
              +
          2 reps one-half up (holding in the half position for 3 seconds)
          2 reps one-half down (holding in the half position for 3 seconds)
              +
          5 full reps

□

15 seconds pause between sets

Set 3: *Triple Iso-Matrix Triad*
          5 full reps
              +
          3 reps one-half up
          3 reps one-half down
              +
          3 reps one-half up (holding in the half position for 3 seconds)
          3 reps one-half down (holding in the half position for 3 seconds)
              +
          5 full reps

□

20 seconds pause between sets

Set 4: *Single Mixed Matrix*
          5 full reps
              +
          1 rep one-fifth up
          1 rep one-half up
              +
          1 rep one-fifth down
          1 rep one-half down
              +
          5 full reps

□

Rest 1 minute between exercises

Exercise C: *Standing Wrist Curl with Barbell Behind the Back*

(Tick the box when you've completed the relevant exercise.)

Set 1: *Single Iso-Matrix Triad*
  5 full reps
    +
  3 reps one-half up
  3 reps one-half down
    +
  1 rep one-half up (holding in the half position for 3 seconds)
  1 rep one-half down (holding in the half position for 3 seconds)
    +
  5 full reps

  ☐

  15 seconds pause between sets

Set 2: *Double Iso-Matrix Triad*
  5 full reps
    +
  3 reps one-half up
  3 reps one-half down
    +
  2 reps one-half up (holding in the half position for 3 seconds)
  2 reps one-half down (holding in the half position for 3 seconds)
    +
  5 full reps

  ☐

  15 seconds pause between sets

Set 3: *Triple Iso-Matrix Triad*
  5 full reps
    +
  3 reps one-half up
  3 reps one-half down
    +
  3 reps one-half up (holding in the half position for 3 seconds)
  3 reps one-half down (holding in the half position for 3 seconds)
    +
  5 full reps

  ☐

  20 seconds pause between sets

Standing Wrist Curl with Barbell Behind
the Back

Set 4: *Single Mixed Matrix*
         5 full reps
              +
         1 rep one-fifth up
         1 rep one-half up
              +
         1 rep one-fifth down
         1 rep one-half down
              +
         5 full reps

         Finish of Tuesday training routine

8   Wednesday training routine (month 1): thighs, calves, abdominals

Thighs

Exercise A: Leg Extension

(Tick the box when you've completed the relevant exercise.)

Set 1: *Single Iso-Matrix Triad*
    5 full reps
        +
    3 reps one-half up
    3 reps one-half down
        +
    1 rep one-half up (holding in the half position for 3 seconds)
    1 rep one-half down (holding in the half position for 3 seconds)
        +
    5 full reps
    ☐

    15 seconds pause between sets

Set 2: *Double Iso-Matrix Triad*
    5 full reps
        +
    3 reps one-half up
    3 reps one-half down
        +
    2 reps one-half up (holding in the half position for 3 seconds)
    2 reps one-half down (holding in the half position for 3 seconds)
        +
    5 full reps
    ☐

    15 seconds pause between sets

Set 3: *Triple Iso-Matrix Triad*
        5 full reps
            +
        3 reps one-half up
        3 reps one-half down
            +
        3 reps one-half up (holding in the half position for 3 seconds)
        3 reps one-half down (holding in the half position for 3 seconds)
            +
        5 full reps

☐

20 seconds pause between sets

Set 4: *Single Mixed Matrix*
        5 full reps
            +
        1 rep one-fifth up
        1 rep one-half up
            +
        1 rep one-fifth down
        1 rep one-half down
            +
        5 full reps

☐

Rest 1 minute between exercises

Exercise B: Hack Squat

(Tick the box when you've completed the relevant exercise.)

Set 1: *Single Iso-Matrix Triad*
        5 full reps
            +
        3 reps one-half up
        3 reps one-half down
            +
        1 rep one-half up (holding in the half position for 3 seconds)
        1 rep one-half down (holding in the half position for 3 seconds)
            +
        5 full reps

☐

15 seconds pause between sets

Set 2: *Double Iso-Matrix Triad*
      5 full reps
        +
      3 reps one-half up
      3 reps one-half down
        +
      2 reps one-half up (holding in the half position for 3 seconds)
      2 reps one-half down (holding in the half position for 3 seconds)
        +
      5 full reps

      15 seconds pause between sets

Set 3: *Triple Iso-Matrix Triad*
      5 full reps
        +
      3 reps one-half up
      3 reps one-half down
        +
      3 reps one-half up (holding in the half position for 3 seconds)
      3 reps one-half down (holding in the half position for 3 seconds)
        +
      5 full reps

      20 seconds pause between sets

Set 4: *Single Mixed Matrix*
      5 full reps
        +
      1 rep one-fifth up
      1 rep one-half up
        +
      1 rep one-fifth down
      1 rep one-half down
        +
      5 full reps

      Rest 1 minute between exercises

Hack Squat

Exercise C: Leg Press

(Tick the box when you've completed the relevant exercise.)

Set 1: *Single Iso-Matrix Triad*
5 full reps
+
3 reps one-half up
3 reps one-half down
+
1 rep one-half up (holding in the half position for 3 seconds)
1 rep one-half down (holding in the half position for 3 seconds)
+
5 full reps

15 seconds pause between sets

Set 2: *Double Iso-Matrix Triad*
    5 full reps
      +
    3 reps one-half up
    3 reps one-half down
      +
    2 reps one-half up (holding in the half position for 3 seconds)
    2 reps one-half down (holding in the half position for 3 seconds)
      +
    5 full reps

☐

    15 seconds pause between sets

Set 3: *Triple Iso-Matrix Triad*
    5 full reps
      +
    3 reps one-half up
    3 reps one-half down
      +
    3 reps one-half up (holding in the half position for 3 seconds)
    3 reps one-half down (holding in the half position for 3 seconds)
      +
    5 full reps

☐

    20 seconds pause between sets

Set 4: *Single Mixed Matrix*
    5 full reps
      +
    1 rep one-fifth up
    1 rep one-half up
      +
    1 rep one-fifth down
    1 rep one-half down
      +
    5 full reps

☐

    Rest 1 minute between exercises

Exercise D: Leg Curls

(Tick the box when you've completed the relevant exercise.)

Set 1: *Single Iso-Matrix Triad*
      5 full reps

       +

      3 reps one-half up
      3 reps one-half down

       +

      1 rep one-half up (holding in the half position for 3 seconds)
      1 rep one-half down (holding in the half position for 3 seconds)

       +

      5 full reps   ☐

15 seconds pause between sets

Set 2: *Double Iso-Matrix Triad*
      5 full reps

       +

      3 reps one-half up
      3 reps one-half down

       +

      2 reps one-half up (holding in the half position for 3 seconds)
      2 reps one-half down (holding in the half position for 3 seconds)

       +

      5 full reps   ☐

15 seconds pause between sets

Set 3: *Triple Iso-Matrix Triad*
      5 full reps

       +

      3 reps one-half up
      3 reps one-half down

       +

      3 reps one-half up (holding in the half position for 3 seconds)
      3 reps one-half down (holding in the half position for 3 seconds)

       +

      5 full reps   ☐

20 seconds pause between sets

Set 4: *Single Mixed Matrix*
5 full reps
+
1 rep one-fifth up
1 rep one-half up
+
1 rep one-fifth down
1 rep one-half down
+
5 full reps

☐

Rest 3 minutes before proceeding to the next body part exercise

Calves

Exercise A: Triceps Pushdowns

(Tick the box when you've completed the relevant exercise.)

Set 1: *Single Iso-Matrix Triad*
5 full reps
+
3 reps one-half up
3 reps one-half down
+
1 rep one-half up (holding in the half position for 3 seconds)
1 rep one-half down (holding in the half position for 3 seconds)
+
5 full reps

☐

15 seconds pause between sets

Set 2: *Double Iso-Matrix Triad*
5 full reps
+
3 reps one-half up
3 reps one-half down
+
2 reps one-half up (holding in the half position for 3 seconds)
2 reps one-half down (holding in the half position for 3 seconds)
+
5 full reps

☐

15 seconds pause between sets

Set 3: *Triple Iso-Matrix Triad*
  5 full reps
     +
  3 reps one-half up
  3 reps one-half down
     +
  3 reps one-half up (holding in the half position for 3 seconds)
  3 reps one-half down (holding in the half position for 3 seconds)
     +
  5 full reps

  ☐

  20 seconds pause between sets

Set 4: *Single Mixed Matrix*
  5 full reps
     +
  1 rep one-fifth up
  1 rep one-half up
     +
  1 rep one-fifth down
  1 rep one-half down
     +
  5 full reps

  ☐

  Rest 1 minute between exercises

Exercise B: Seated Calf Raises

(Tick the box when you've completed the relevant exercise.)

Set 1: *Single Iso-Matrix Triad*
  5 full reps
     +
  3 reps one-half up
  3 reps one-half down
     +
  1 rep one-half up (holding in the half position for 3 seconds)
  1 rep one-half down (holding in the half position for 3 seconds)
     +
  5 full reps

  ☐

  15 seconds pause between sets

Seated Calf Raise

Set 2: *Double Iso-Matrix Triad*
5 full reps
+
3 reps one-half up
3 reps one-half down
+
2 reps one-half up (holding in the half position for 3 seconds)
2 reps one-half down (holding in the half position for 3 seconds)
+
5 full reps

15 seconds pause between sets

Set 3: *Triple Iso-Matrix Triad*
5 full reps
+
3 reps one-half up
3 reps one-half down
+
3 reps one-half up (holding in the half position for 3 seconds)
3 reps one-half down (holding in the half position for 3 seconds)
+
5 full reps

20 seconds pause between sets

Set 4: *Single Mixed Matrix*
        5 full reps
          +
        1 rep one-fifth up
        1 rep one-half up
          +
        1 rep one-fifth down
        1 rep one-half down
          +
        5 full reps

☐

Rest 1 minute between exercises

Exercise C: One-leg Calf Raises

(Tick the box when you've completed the relevant exercise.)

Set 1: *Single Iso-Matrix Triad*
        5 full reps
          +
        3 reps one-half up
        3 reps one-half down
          +
        1 rep one-half up (holding in the half position for 3 seconds)
        1 rep one-half down (holding in the half position for 3 seconds)
          +
        5 full reps

☐

15 seconds pause between sets

Set 2: *Double Iso-Matrix Triad*
        5 full reps
          +
        3 reps one-half up
        3 reps one-half down
          +
        2 reps one-half up (holding in the half position for 3 seconds)
        2 reps one-half down (holding in the half position for 3 seconds)
          +
        5 full reps

☐

15 seconds pause between sets

Set 3: *Triple Iso-Matrix Triad*
        5 full reps
         +
        3 reps one-half up
        3 reps one-half down
         +
        3 reps one-half up (holding in the half position for 3 seconds)
        3 reps one-half down (holding in the half position for 3 seconds)
         +
        5 full reps

☐

20 seconds pause between sets

Set 4: *Single Mixed Matrix*
        5 full reps
         +
        1 rep one-fifth up
        1 rep one-half up
         +
        1 rep one-fifth down
        1 rep one-half down
         +
        5 full reps

☐

Rest 3 minutes before proceeding to the next body part exercise

Abdominals

Exercise A: Bent-knee Hanging Leg Raises

(Tick the box when you've completed the relevant exercise.)

Set 1: *Single Iso-Matrix Triad*
        5 full reps
         +
        3 reps one-half up
        3 reps one-half down
         +
        1 rep one-half up (holding in the half position for 3 seconds)
        1 rep one-half down (holding in the half position for 3 seconds)
         +
        5 full reps

☐

15 seconds pause between sets

Hanging Leg Raise

Set 2: *Double Iso-Matrix Triad*
        5 full reps
            +
        3 reps one-half up
        3 reps one-half down
            +
        2 reps one-half up (holding in the half position for 3 seconds)
        2 reps one-half down (holding in the half position for 3 seconds)
            +
        5 full reps

        15 seconds pause between sets

Set 3: *Triple Iso-Matrix Triad*
        5 full reps
            +
        3 reps one-half up
        3 reps one-half down
            +
        3 reps one-half up (holding in the half position for 3 seconds)
        3 reps one-half down (holding in the half position for 3 seconds)
            +
        5 full reps

        20 seconds pause between sets

Set 4: *Single Mixed Matrix*
          5 full reps
            +
          1 rep one-fifth up
          1 rep one-half up
            +
          1 rep one-fifth down
          1 rep one-half down
            +
          5 full reps

☐

Rest 1 minute between exercises

Exercise B: Crunches

(Tick the box when you've completed the relevant exercise.)

Set 1: *Single Iso-Matrix Triad*
          5 full reps
            +
          3 reps one-half up
          3 reps one-half down
            +
          1 rep one-half up (holding in the half position for 3 seconds)
          1 rep one-half down (holding in the half position for 3 seconds)
            +
          5 full reps

☐

15 seconds pause between sets

Set 2: *Double Iso-Matrix Triad*
          5 full reps
            +
          3 reps one-half up
          3 reps one-half down
            +
          2 reps one-half up (holding in the half position for 3 seconds)
          2 reps one-half down (holding in the half position for 3 seconds)
            +
          5 full reps

☐

15 seconds pause between sets

Set 3: *Triple Iso-Matrix Triad*
        5 full reps
           +
        3 reps one-half up
        3 reps one-half down
           +
        3 reps one-half up (holding in the half position for 3 seconds)
        3 reps one-half down (holding in the half position for 3 seconds)
           +
        5 full reps

☐

        20 seconds pause between sets

Set 4: *Single Mixed Matrix*
        5 full reps
           +
        1 rep one-fifth up
        1 rep one-half up
           +
        1 rep one-fifth down
        1 rep one-half down
           +
        5 full reps

☐

        Rest 1 minute between exercises

Exercise C: Bent-knee Incline Board Raises

(Tick the box when you've completed the relevant exercise.)

Set 1: *Single Iso-Matrix Triad*
        5 full reps
           +
        3 reps one-half up
        3 reps one-half down
           +
        1 rep one-half up (holding in the half position for 3 seconds)
        1 rep one-half down (holding in the half position for 3 seconds)
           +
        5 full reps

☐

        15 seconds pause between sets

Set 2: *Double Iso-Matrix Triad*
5 full reps
+
3 reps one-half up
3 reps one-half down
+
2 reps one-half up (holding in the half position for 3 seconds)
2 reps one-half down (holding in the half position for 3 seconds)
+
5 full reps

☐

15 seconds pause between sets

Set 3: *Triple Iso-Matrix Triad*
5 full reps
+
3 reps one-half up
3 reps one-half down
+
3 reps one-half up (holding in the half position for 3 seconds)
3 reps one-half down (holding in the half position for 3 seconds)
+
5 full reps

☐

20 seconds pause between sets

Set 4: *Single Mixed Matrix*
5 full reps
+
1 rep one-fifth up
1 rep one-half up
+
1 rep one-fifth down
1 rep one-half down
+
5 full reps

☐

Finish of Wednesday training routine

9 Thursday training routine (month 1): upper back and lower back

Upper back

Exercise A: Lat Machine Pulldowns behind the Neck

Note: change grip on bar with every set.
(Tick the box when you've completed the relevant exercise.)

Set 1: *Single Iso-Matrix Triad*
    5 full reps
      +
    3 reps one-half up
    3 reps one-half down
      +
    1 rep one-half up (holding in the half position for 3 seconds)
    1 rep one-half down (holding in the half position for 3 seconds)
      +
    5 full reps
          ☐

    15 seconds pause between sets

Set 2: *Double Iso-Matrix Triad*
    5 full reps
      +
    3 reps one-half up
    3 reps one-half down
      +
    2 reps one-half up (holding in the half position for 3 seconds)
    2 reps one-half down (holding in the half position for 3 seconds)
      +
    5 full reps
          ☐

    15 seconds pause between sets

Set 3: *Triple Iso-Matrix Triad*
     5 full reps
       +
     3 reps one-half up
     3 reps one-half down
       +
     3 reps one-half up (holding in the half position for 3 seconds)
     3 reps one-half down (holding in the half position for 3 seconds)
       +
     5 full reps

     ☐

     20 seconds pause between sets

Set 4: *Single Mixed Matrix*
     5 full reps
       +
     1 rep one-fifth up
     1 rep one-half up
       +
     1 rep one-fifth down
     1 rep one-half down
       +
     5 full reps

     ☐

     Rest 1 minute between exercises

Exercise B: Bent over Barbell Rows

(Tick the box when you've completed the relevant exercise.)

Set 1: *Single Iso-Matrix Triad*
     5 full reps
       +
     3 reps one-half up
     3 reps one-half down
       +
     1 rep one-half up (holding in the half position for 3 seconds)
     1 rep one-half down (holding in the half position for 3 seconds)
       +
     5 full reps

     ☐

     15 seconds pause between sets

Set 2: *Double Iso-Matrix Triad*
        5 full reps
          +
        3 reps one-half up
        3 reps one-half down
          +
        2 reps one-half up (holding in the half position for 3 seconds)
        2 reps one-half down (holding in the half position for 3 seconds)
          +
        5 full reps

⬜

        15 seconds pause between sets

Set 3: *Triple Iso-Matrix Triad*
        5 full reps
          +
        3 reps one-half up
        3 reps one-half down
          +
        3 reps one-half up (holding in the half position for 3 seconds)
        3 reps one-half down (holding in the half position for 3 seconds)
          +
        5 full reps

⬜

        20 seconds pause between sets

Set 4: *Single Mixed Matrix*
        5 full reps
          +
        1 rep one-fifth up
        1 rep one-half up
          +
        1 rep one-fifth down
        1 rep one-half down
          +
        5 full reps

⬜

        Rest 1 minute between exercises

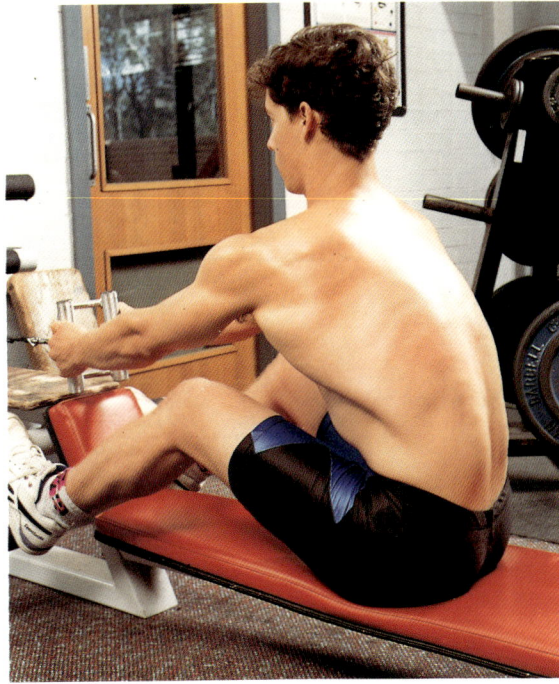

Seated Cable Row

Exercise C: Seated Cable Row

(Tick the box when you've completed the relevant exercise.)

Set 1: *Single Iso-Matrix Triad*
        5 full reps
            +
        3 reps one-half up
        3 reps one-half down
            +
        1 rep one-half up (holding in the half position for 3 seconds)
        1 rep one-half down (holding in the half position for 3 seconds)
            +
        5 full reps

☐

15 seconds pause between sets

Set 2: *Double Iso-Matrix Triad*
   5 full reps
    +
   3 reps one-half up
   3 reps one-half down
    +
   2 reps one-half up (holding in the half position for 3 seconds)
   2 reps one-half down (holding in the half position for 3 seconds)
    +
   5 full reps

   15 seconds pause between sets

Set 3: *Triple Iso-Matrix Triad*
   5 full reps
    +
   3 reps one-half up
   3 reps one-half down
    +
   3 reps one-half up (holding in the half position for 3 seconds)
   3 reps one-half down (holding in the half position for 3 seconds)
    +
   5 full reps

   20 seconds pause between sets

Set 4: *Single Mixed Matrix*
   5 full reps
    +
   1 rep one-fifth up
   1 rep one-half up
    +
   1 rep one-fifth down
   1 rep one-half down
    +
   5 full reps

   Rest 1 minute between exercises

Exercise D: Lat Machine Pulldowns in front of Neck

Note: Change grip on bar with every set.
(Tick the box when you've completed the relevant exercise.)

Set 1: *Single Iso-Matrix Triad*
         5 full reps
            +
         3 reps one-half up
         3 reps one-half down
            +
         1 rep one-half up (holding in the half position for 3 seconds)
         1 rep one-half down (holding in the half position for 3 seconds)
            +
         5 full reps   ☐

         15 seconds pause between sets

Set 2: *Double Iso-Matrix Triad*
         5 full reps
            +
         3 reps one-half up
         3 reps one-half down
            +
         2 reps one-half up (holding in the half position for 3 seconds)
         2 reps one-half down (holding in the half position for 3 seconds)
            +
         5 full reps   ☐

         15 seconds pause between sets

Set 3: *Triple Iso-Matrix Triad*
         5 full reps
            +
         3 reps one-half up
         3 reps one-half down
            +
         3 reps one-half up (holding in the half position for 3 seconds)
         3 reps one-half down (holding in the half position for 3 seconds)
            +
         5 full reps   ☐

         20 seconds pause between sets

Set 4:   *Single Mixed Matrix*
5 full reps
+
1 rep one-fifth up
1 rep one-half up
+
1 rep one-fifth down
1 rep one-half down
+
5 full reps

☐

Rest 3 minutes before proceeding to the next body part exercise

Lower back

Exercise A: Hyperextensions

(Tick the box when you've completed the relevant exercise.)

Set 1:   *Single Iso-Matrix Triad*
5 full reps
+
3 reps one-half up
3 reps one-half down
+
1 rep one-half up (holding in the half position for 3 seconds)
1 rep one-half down (holding in the half position for 3 seconds)
+
5 full reps

☐

15 seconds pause between sets

Set 2:   *Double Iso-Matrix Triad*
5 full reps
+
3 reps one-half up
3 reps one-half down
+
2 reps one-half up (holding in the half position for 3 seconds)
2 reps one-half down (holding in the half position for 3 seconds)
+
5 full reps

☐

15 seconds pause between sets

Hyperextension

Set 3: *Triple Iso-Matrix Triad*
5 full reps
+
3 reps one-half up
3 reps one-half down
+
3 reps one-half up (holding in the half position for 3 seconds)
3 reps one-half down (holding in the half position for 3 seconds)
+
5 full reps

☐

20 seconds pause between sets

Set 4: *Single Mixed Matrix*
5 full reps
+
1 rep one-fifth up
1 rep one-half up
+
1 rep one-fifth down
1 rep one-half down
+
5 full reps

☐

Rest 1 minute between exercises

Exercise B: T-bar Rows

(Tick the box when you've completed the relevant exercise.)

Set 1: *Single Iso-Matrix Triad*
      5 full reps
       +
      3 reps one-half up
      3 reps one-half down
       +
      1 rep one-half up (holding in the half position for 3 seconds)
      1 rep one-half down (holding in the half position for 3 seconds)
       +
      5 full reps ☐

      15 seconds pause between sets

Set 2: *Double Iso-Matrix Triad*
      5 full reps
       +
      3 reps one-half up
      3 reps one-half down
       +
      2 reps one-half up (holding in the half position for 3 seconds)
      2 reps one-half down (holding in the half position for 3 seconds)
       +
      5 full reps ☐

      15 seconds pause between sets

Set 3: *Triple Iso-Matrix Triad*
      5 full reps
       +
      3 reps one-half up
      3 reps one-half down
       +
      3 reps one-half up (holding in the half position for 3 seconds)
      3 reps one-half down (holding in the half position for 3 seconds)
       +
      5 full reps ☐

      20 seconds pause between sets

Set 4: *Single Mixed Matrix*
    5 full reps
       +
    1 rep one-fifth up
    1 rep one-half up
       +
    1 rep one-fifth down
    1 rep one-half down
       +
    5 full reps

☐

Rest 1 minute between exercises

Exercise C: Good Mornings with Knees Bent

(Tick the box when you've completed the relevant exercise.)

Set 1: *Single Iso-Matrix Triad*
    5 full reps
       +
    3 reps one-half up
    3 reps one-half down
       +
    1 rep one-half up (holding in the half position for 3 seconds)
    1 rep one-half down (holding in the half position for 3 seconds)
       +
    5 full reps

☐

15 seconds pause between sets

Set 2: *Double Iso-Matrix Triad*
    5 full reps
       +
    3 reps one-half up
    3 reps one-half down
       +
    2 reps one-half up (holding in the half position for 3 seconds)
    2 reps one-half down (holding in the half position for 3 seconds)
       +
    5 full reps

☐

15 seconds pause between sets

Good Morning with Knees Bent

Set 3: *Triple Iso-Matrix Triad*
     5 full reps
         +
     3 reps one-half up
     3 reps one-half down
         +
     3 reps one-half up (holding in the half position for 3 seconds)
     3 reps one-half down (holding in the half position for 3 seconds)
         +
     5 full reps

     20 seconds pause between sets

Set 4: *Single Mixed Matrix*
     5 full reps
         +
     1 rep one-fifth up
     1 rep one-half up
         +
     1 rep one-fifth down
     1 rep one-half down
         +
     5 full reps

     Finish of Thursday training routine

10 Friday training routine (month 1): biceps, triceps, forearms and calves

Biceps

Exercise A: Two-hand Standing Cable Curls with Bar

(Tick the box when you've completed the relevant exercise.)

Set 1: *Single Iso-Matrix Triad*
5 full reps
+
3 reps one-half up
3 reps one-half down
+
1 rep one-half up (holding in the half position for 3 seconds)
1 rep one-half down (holding in the half position for 3 seconds)
+
5 full reps ☐

15 seconds pause between sets

Set 2: *Double Iso-Matrix Triad*
5 full reps
+
3 reps one-half up
3 reps one-half down
+
2 reps one-half up (holding in the half position for 3 seconds)
2 reps one-half down (holding in the half position for 3 seconds)
+
5 full reps ☐

15 seconds pause between sets

Set 3: *Triple Iso-Matrix Triad*
5 full reps
+
3 reps one-half up
3 reps one-half down
+
3 reps one-half up (holding in the half position for 3 seconds)
3 reps one-half down (holding in the half position for 3 seconds)
+
5 full reps

20 seconds pause between sets

Set 4: *Single Mixed Matrix*
5 full reps
+
1 rep one-fifth up
1 rep one-half up
+
1 rep one-fifth down
1 rep one-half down
+
5 full reps

Rest 1 minute between exercises

Exercise B: Seated Dumbbell Curls

(Tick the box when you've completed the relevant exercise.)

Set 1: *Single Iso-Matrix Triad*
5 full reps
+
3 reps one-half up
3 reps one-half down
+
1 rep one-half up (holding in the half position for 3 seconds)
1 rep one-half down (holding in the half position for 3 seconds)
+
5 full reps

15 seconds pause between sets

Standing Cable Curls with Bar

Set 2: *Double Iso-Matrix Triad*
    5 full reps
      +
    3 reps one-half up
    3 reps one-half down
      +
    2 reps one-half up (holding in the half position for 3 seconds)
    2 reps one-half down (holding in the half position for 3 seconds)
      +
    5 full reps

15 seconds pause between sets

Set 3: *Triple Iso-Matrix Triad*
    5 full reps
        +
    3 reps one-half up
    3 reps one-half down
        +
    3 reps one-half up (holding in the half position for 3 seconds)
    3 reps one-half down (holding in the half position for 3 seconds)
        +
    5 full reps

□

20 seconds pause between sets

Set 4: *Single Mixed Matrix*
    5 full reps
        +
    1 rep one-fifth up
    1 rep one-half up
        +
    1 rep one-fifth down
    1 rep one-half down
        +
    5 full reps

□

Rest 1 minute between exercises

Exercise C: Concentration Curls with Dumbbell

(Tick the box when you've completed the relevant exercise.)

Set 1: *Single Iso-Matrix Triad*
    5 full reps
        +
    3 reps one-half up
    3 reps one-half down
        +
    1 rep one-half up (holding in the half position for 3 seconds)
    1 rep one-half down (holding in the half position for 3 seconds)
        +
    5 full reps

□

15 seconds pause between sets

Set 2: *Double Iso-Matrix Triad*
　　　　5 full reps
　　　　　+
　　　　3 reps one-half up
　　　　3 reps one-half down
　　　　　+
　　　　2 reps one-half up (holding in the half position for 3 seconds)
　　　　2 reps one-half down (holding in the half position for 3 seconds)
　　　　　+
　　　　5 full reps

☐

　　　　15 seconds pause between sets

Set 3: *Triple Iso-Matrix Triad*
　　　　5 full reps
　　　　　+
　　　　3 reps one-half up
　　　　3 reps one-half down
　　　　　+
　　　　3 reps one-half up (holding in the half position for 3 seconds)
　　　　3 reps one-half down (holding in the half position for 3 seconds)
　　　　　+
　　　　5 full reps

☐

　　　　20 seconds pause between sets

Set 4: *Single Mixed Matrix*
　　　　5 full reps
　　　　　+
　　　　1 rep one-fifth up
　　　　1 rep one-half up
　　　　　+
　　　　1 rep one-fifth down
　　　　1 rep one-half down
　　　　　+
　　　　5 full reps

☐

　　　　Rest 3 minutes before proceeding to the next body part exercise

One-arm Cable
Reverse Pressdowns

Triceps

Exercise A: One-arm Cable Reverse Pressdowns

(Tick the box when you've completed the relevant exercise.)

Set 1: *Single Iso-Matrix Triad*
5 full reps
+
3 reps one-half up
3 reps one-half down
+
1 rep one-half up (holding in the half position for 3 seconds)
1 rep one-half down (holding in the half position for 3 seconds)
+
5 full reps

☐

15 seconds pause between sets

Set 2: *Double Iso-Matrix Triad*
 5 full reps
   +
 3 reps one-half up
 3 reps one-half down
   +
 2 reps one-half up (holding in the half position for 3 seconds)
 2 reps one-half down (holding in the half position for 3 seconds)
   +
 5 full reps

☐

 15 seconds pause between sets

Set 3: *Triple Iso-Matrix Triad*
 5 full reps
   +
 3 reps one-half up
 3 reps one-half down
   +
 3 reps one-half up (holding in the half position for 3 seconds)
 3 reps one-half down (holding in the half position for 3 seconds)
   +
 5 full reps

☐

 20 seconds pause between sets

Set 4: *Single Mixed Matrix*
 5 full reps
   +
 1 rep one-fifth up
 1 rep one-half up
   +
 1 rep one-fifth down
 1 rep one-half down
   +
 5 full reps

☐

 Rest 1 minute between exercises

Exercise B: Dumbbell Kickbacks

(Tick the box when you've completed the relevant exercise.)

Set 1: *Single Iso-Matrix Triad*
      5 full reps
       +
      3 reps one-half up
      3 reps one-half down
       +
      1 rep one-half up (holding in the half position for 3 seconds)
      1 rep one-half down (holding in the half position for 3 seconds)
       +
      5 full reps

      15 seconds pause between sets

Set 2: *Double Iso-Matrix Triad*
      5 full reps
       +
      3 reps one-half up
      3 reps one-half down
       +
      2 reps one-half up (holding in the half position for 3 seconds)
      2 reps one-half down (holding in the half position for 3 seconds)
       +
      5 full reps

      15 seconds pause between sets

Set 3: *Triple Iso-Matrix Triad*
      5 full reps
       +
      3 reps one-half up
      3 reps one-half down
       +
      3 reps one-half up (holding in the half position for 3 seconds)
      3 reps one-half down (holding in the half position for 3 seconds)
       +
      5 full reps

      20 seconds pause between sets

Set 4: *Single Mixed Matrix*
        5 full reps
            +
        1 rep one-fifth up
        1 rep one-half up
            +
        1 rep one-fifth down
        1 rep one-half down
            +
        5 full reps

Rest 1 minute between exercises

Exercise C: Lying Cross Face Triceps Extensions

(Tick the box when you've completed the relevant exercise.)

Set 1: *Single Iso-Matrix Triad*
        5 full reps
            +
        3 reps one-half up
        3 reps one-half down
            +
        1 rep one-half up (holding in the half position for 3 seconds)
        1 rep one-half down (holding in the half position for 3 seconds)
            +
        5 full reps

15 seconds pause between sets

Set 2: *Double Iso-Matrix Triad*
        5 full reps
            +
        3 reps one-half up
        3 reps one-half down
            +
        2 reps one-half up (holding in the half position for 3 seconds)
        2 reps one-half down (holding in the half position for 3 seconds)
            +
        5 full reps

15 seconds pause between sets

Adam Laura shares a
common commitment to
Matrix training with his father,
Professor Ronald Laura

Set 3:   *Triple Iso-Matrix Triad*
   5 full reps
      +
   3 reps one-half up
   3 reps one-half down
      +
   3 reps one-half up (holding in the half position for 3 seconds)
   3 reps one-half down (holding in the half position for 3 seconds)
      +
   5 full reps

   20 seconds pause between sets

Set 4: *Single Mixed Matrix*
  5 full reps
    +
  1 rep one-fifth up
  1 rep one-half up
    +
  1 rep one-fifth down
  1 rep one-half down
    +
  5 full reps

☐

Rest 3 minutes before proceeding to the next body part exercise

Forearms

Exercise A: Reverse Preacher Bench Barbell Curls

(Tick the box when you've completed the relevant exercise.)

Set 1: *Single Iso-Matrix Triad*
  5 full reps
    +
  3 reps one-half up
  3 reps one-half down
    +
  1 rep one-half up (holding in the half position for 3 seconds)
  1 rep one-half down (holding in the half position for 3 seconds)
    +
  5 full reps

☐

15 seconds pause between sets

Set 2: *Double Iso-Matrix Triad*
  5 full reps
    +
  3 reps one-half up
  3 reps one-half down
    +
  2 reps one-half up (holding in the half position for 3 seconds)
  2 reps one-half down (holding in the half position for 3 seconds)
    +
  5 full reps

☐

15 seconds pause between sets

Set 3:   *Triple Iso-Matrix Triad*
          5 full reps
             +
          3 reps one-half up
          3 reps one-half down
             +
          3 reps one-half up (holding in the half position for 3 seconds)
          3 reps one-half down (holding in the half position for 3 seconds)
             +
          5 full reps

☐

   20 seconds pause between sets

Set 4:   *Single Mixed Matrix*
          5 full reps
             +
          1 rep one-fifth up
          1 rep one-half up
             +
          1 rep one-fifth down
          1 rep one-half down
             +
          5 full reps

☐

   Rest 1 minute between exercises

Exercise B: Seated Wrist Curl with Barbell

(Tick the box when you've completed the relevant exercise.)

Set 1:   *Single Iso-Matrix Triad*
          5 full reps
             +
          3 reps one-half up
          3 reps one-half down
             +
          1 rep one-half up (holding in the half position for 3 seconds)
          1 rep one-half down (holding in the half position for 3 seconds)
             +
          5 full reps

☐

   15 seconds pause between sets

Set 2: *Double Iso-Matrix Triad*
        5 full reps
            +
        3 reps one-half up
        3 reps one-half down
            +
        2 reps one-half up (holding in the half position for 3 seconds)
        2 reps one-half down (holding in the half position for 3 seconds)
            +
        5 full reps

        □

15 seconds pause between sets

Set 3: *Triple Iso-Matrix Triad*
        5 full reps
            +
        3 reps one-half up
        3 reps one-half down
            +
        3 reps one-half up (holding in the half position for 3 seconds)
        3 reps one-half down (holding in the half position for 3 seconds)
            +
        5 full reps

        □

20 seconds pause between sets

Set 4: *Single Mixed Matrix*
        5 full reps
            +
        1 rep one-fifth up
        1 rep one-half up
            +
        1 rep one-fifth down
        1 rep one-half down
            +
        5 full reps

        □

Rest 1 minute between exercises

Exercise C: Standing One-arm Cable Reverse Curls

(Tick the box when you've completed the relevant exercise.)

Set 1: *Single Iso-Matrix Triad*
        5 full reps
            +
        3 reps one-half up
        3 reps one-half down
            +
        1 rep one-half up (holding in the half position for 3 seconds)
        1 rep one-half down (holding in the half position for 3 seconds)
            +
        5 full reps

       □

       15 seconds pause between sets

Set 2: *Double Iso-Matrix Triad*
        5 full reps
            +
        3 reps one-half up
        3 reps one-half down
            +
        2 reps one-half up (holding in the half position for 3 seconds)
        2 reps one-half down (holding in the half position for 3 seconds)
            +
        5 full reps

       □

       15 seconds pause between sets

Set 3: *Triple Iso-Matrix Triad*
        5 full reps
            +
        3 reps one-half up
        3 reps one-half down
            +
        3 reps one-half up (holding in the half position for 3 seconds)
        3 reps one-half down (holding in the half position for 3 seconds)
            +
        5 full reps

       □

       20 seconds pause between sets

Standing Calf Raises

Set 4: *Single Mixed Matrix*
        5 full reps
          +
        1 rep one-fifth up
        1 rep one-half up
          +
        1 rep one-fifth down
        1 rep one-half down
          +
        5 full reps

        Rest 1 minute between exercises

Calves

Exercise A: Donkey Calf Raises

(Tick the box when you've completed the relevant exercise.)

Set 1: *Single Iso-Matrix Triad*
5 full reps
    +
3 reps one-half up
3 reps one-half down
    +
1 rep one-half up (holding in the half position for 3 seconds)
1 rep one-half down (holding in the half position for 3 seconds)
    +
5 full reps

☐

15 seconds pause between sets

Set 2: *Double Iso-Matrix Triad*
5 full reps
    +
3 reps one-half up
3 reps one-half down
    +
2 reps one-half up (holding in the half position for 3 seconds)
2 reps one-half down (holding in the half position for 3 seconds)
    +
5 full reps

☐

15 seconds pause between sets

Set 3: *Triple Iso-Matrix Triad*
5 full reps
    +
3 reps one-half up
3 reps one-half down
    +
3 reps one-half up (holding in the half position for 3 seconds)
3 reps one-half down (holding in the half position for 3 seconds)
    +
5 full reps

☐

20 seconds pause between sets

Set 4: *Single Mixed Matrix*
   5 full reps
      +
   1 rep one-fifth up
   1 rep one-half up
      +
   1 rep one-fifth down
   1 rep one-half down
      +
   5 full reps

☐

Rest 1 minute between exercises

Exercise B: Reverse Calf Raises

(Tick the box when you've completed the relevant exercise.)

Set 1: *Single Iso-Matrix Triad*
   5 full reps
      +
   3 reps one-half up
   3 reps one-half down
      +
   1 rep one-half up (holding in the half position for 3 seconds)
   1 rep one-half down (holding in the half position for 3 seconds)
      +
   5 full reps

☐

15 seconds pause between sets

Set 2: *Double Iso-Matrix Triad*
   5 full reps
      +
   3 reps one-half up
   3 reps one-half down
      +
   2 reps one-half up (holding in the half position for 3 seconds)
   2 reps one-half down (holding in the half position for 3 seconds)
      +
   5 full reps

☐

15 seconds pause between sets

Set 3: *Triple Iso-Matrix Triad*
        5 full reps
            +
        3 reps one-half up
        3 reps one-half down
            +
        3 reps one-half up (holding in the half position for 3 seconds)
        3 reps one-half down (holding in the half position for 3 seconds)
            +
        5 full reps

☐

20 seconds pause between sets

Set 4: *Single Mixed Matrix*
        5 full reps
            +
        1 rep one-fifth up
        1 rep one-half up
            +
        1 rep one-fifth down
        1 rep one-half down
            +
        5 full reps

☐

Rest 1 minute between exercises

Exercise C: Calf Raises on Leg Press Machine

(Tick the box when you've completed the relevant exercise.)

Set 1: *Single Iso-Matrix Triad*
        5 full reps
            +
        3 reps one-half up
        3 reps one-half down
            +
        1 rep one-half up (holding in the half position for 3 seconds)
        1 rep one-half down (holding in the half position for 3 seconds)
            +
        5 full reps

☐

15 seconds pause between sets

Set 2: *Double Iso-Matrix Triad*
    5 full reps
        +
    3 reps one-half up
    3 reps one-half down
        +
    2 reps one-half up (holding in the half position for 3 seconds)
    2 reps one-half down (holding in the half position for 3 seconds)
        +
    5 full reps

⬜

15 seconds pause between sets

Set 3: *Triple Iso-Matrix Triad*
    5 full reps
        +
    3 reps one-half up
    3 reps one-half down
        +
    3 reps one-half up (holding in the half position for 3 seconds)
    3 reps one-half down (holding in the half position for 3 seconds)
        +
    5 full reps

⬜

20 seconds pause between sets

Set 4: *Single Mixed Matrix*
    5 full reps
        +
    1 rep one-fifth up
    1 rep one-half up
        +
    1 rep one-fifth down
    1 rep one-half down
        +
    5 full reps

⬜

Finish of Friday training routine

11 Saturday training routine (month 1): chest, shoulders and abdominals

Chest

Exercise A: Standing Cable Flyes

(Tick the box when you've completed the relevant exercise.)

Set 1: *Single Iso-Matrix Triad*
    5 full reps
    +
    3 reps one-half up
    3 reps one-half down
    +
    1 rep one-half up (holding in the half position for 3 seconds)
    1 rep one-half down (holding in the half position for 3 seconds)
    +
    5 full reps

☐

    15 seconds pause between sets

Set 2: *Double Iso-Matrix Triad*
    5 full reps
    +
    3 reps one-half up
    3 reps one-half down
    +
    2 reps one-half up (holding in the half position for 3 seconds)
    2 reps one-half down (holding in the half position for 3 seconds)
    +
    5 full reps

☐

    15 seconds pause between sets

Anthony Wingett's superb physique is the result of years of dedicated training.

Set 3: *Triple Iso-Matrix Triad*

5 full reps

+

3 reps one-half up

3 reps one-half down

+

3 reps one-half up (holding in the half position for 3 seconds)

3 reps one-half down (holding in the half position for 3 seconds)

+

5 full reps

20 seconds pause between sets

Set 4:   *Single Mixed Matrix*
   5 full reps
      +
   1 rep one-fifth up
   1 rep one-half up
      +
   1 rep one-fifth down
   1 rep one-half down
      +
   5 full reps

☐

Rest 1 minute between exercises

Exercise B: Parallel Bar Dips

(Tick the box when you've completed the relevant exercise.)

Set 1:   *Single Iso-Matrix Triad*
   5 full reps
      +
   3 reps one-half up
   3 reps one-half down
      +
   1 rep one-half up (holding in the half position for 3 seconds)
   1 rep one-half down (holding in the half position for 3 seconds)
      +
   5 full reps

☐

15 seconds pause between sets

Set 2:   *Double Iso-Matrix Triad*
   5 full reps
      +
   3 reps one-half up
   3 reps one-half down
      +
   2 reps one-half up (holding in the half position for 3 seconds)
   2 reps one-half down (holding in the half position for 3 seconds)
      +
   5 full reps

☐

15 seconds pause between sets

Set 3: *Triple Iso-Matrix Triad*
        5 full reps
          +
        3 reps one-half up
        3 reps one-half down
          +
        3 reps one-half up (holding in the half position for 3 seconds)
        3 reps one-half down (holding in the half position for 3 seconds)
          +
        5 full reps

☐

20 seconds pause between sets

Set 4: *Single Mixed Matrix*
        5 full reps
          +
        1 rep one-fifth up
        1 rep one-half up
          +
        1 rep one-fifth down
        1 rep one-half down
          +
        5 full reps

☐

Rest 1 minute between exercises

Exercise C: Decline Dumbbell Presses

(Tick the box when you've completed the relevant exercise.)

Set 1: *Single Iso-Matrix Triad*
        5 full reps
          +
        3 reps one-half up
        3 reps one-half down
          +
        1 rep one-half up (holding in the half position for 3 seconds)
        1 rep one-half down (holding in the half position for 3 seconds)
          +
        5 full reps

☐

15 seconds pause between sets

Set 2: *Double Iso-Matrix Triad*
5 full reps
+
3 reps one-half up
3 reps one-half down
+
2 reps one-half up (holding in the half position for 3 seconds)
2 reps one-half down (holding in the half position for 3 seconds)
+
5 full reps

□

15 seconds pause between sets

Set 3: *Triple Iso-Matrix Triad*
5 full reps
+
3 reps one-half up
3 reps one-half down
+
3 reps one-half up (holding in the half position for 3 seconds)
3 reps one-half down (holding in the half position for 3 seconds)
+
5 full reps

□

20 seconds pause between sets

Set 4: *Single Mixed Matrix*
5 full reps
+
1 rep one-fifth up
1 rep one-half up
+
1 rep one-fifth down
1 rep one-half down
+
5 full reps

□

Rest 1 minute between exercises

Incline Bench Press on Smith Machine

Exercise D: Incline Bench Press with Barbell

(Tick the box when you've completed the relevant exercise.)

Set 1: *Single Iso-Matrix Triad*
        5 full reps
           +
        3 reps one-half up
        3 reps one-half down
           +
        1 rep one-half up (holding in the half position for 3 seconds)
        1 rep one-half down (holding in the half position for 3 seconds)
           +
        5 full reps

⬜

15 seconds pause between sets

Set 2: *Double Iso-Matrix Triad*
   5 full reps
      +
   3 reps one-half up
   3 reps one-half down
      +
   2 reps one-half up (holding in the half position for 3 seconds)
   2 reps one-half down (holding in the half position for 3 seconds)
      +
   5 full reps

   ☐

   15 seconds pause between sets

Set 3: *Triple Iso-Matrix Triad*
   5 full reps
      +
   3 reps one-half up
   3 reps one-half down
      +
   3 reps one-half up (holding in the half position for 3 seconds)
   3 reps one-half down (holding in the half position for 3 seconds)
      +
   5 full reps

   ☐

   20 seconds pause between sets

Set 4: *Single Mixed Matrix*
   5 full reps
      +
   1 rep one-fifth up
   1 rep one-half up
      +
   1 rep one-fifth down
   1 rep one-half down
      +
   5 full reps

   ☐

   Rest 3 minutes before proceeding to the next body part exercise

Shoulders

Exercise A: Seated Bent-over Dumbbell Laterals

(Tick the box when you've completed the relevant exercise.)

Set 1:   *Single Iso-Matrix Triad*
          5 full reps
             +
          3 reps one-half up
          3 reps one-half down
             +
          1 rep one-half up (holding in the half position for 3 seconds)
          1 rep one-half down (holding in the half position for 3 seconds)
             +
          5 full reps

☐

15 seconds pause between sets

Set 2:   *Double Iso-Matrix Triad*
          5 full reps
             +
          3 reps one-half up
          3 reps one-half down
             +
          2 reps one-half up (holding in the half position for 3 seconds)
          2 reps one-half down (holding in the half position for 3 seconds)
             +
          5 full reps

☐

15 seconds pause between sets

Set 3:   *Triple Iso-Matrix Triad*
          5 full reps
             +
          3 reps one-half up
          3 reps one-half down
             +
          3 reps one-half up (holding in the half position for 3 seconds)
          3 reps one-half down (holding in the half position for 3 seconds)
             +
          5 full reps

☐

20 seconds pause between sets

Seated Bent-Over Dumbbell
Laterals on Cable Machine

Set 4: *Single Mixed Matrix*
5 full reps
+
1 rep one-fifth up
1 rep one-half up
+
1 rep one-fifth down
1 rep one-half down
+
5 full reps

Rest 1 minute between exercises

Upright Rows (starting position)

Exercise B: Upright Rows

(Tick the box when you've completed the relevant exercise.)

Set 1: *Single Iso-Matrix Triad*
        5 full reps
         +
        3 reps one-half up
        3 reps one-half down
         +
        1 rep one-half up (holding in the half position for 3 seconds)
        1 rep one-half down (holding in the half position for 3 seconds)
         +
        5 full reps   ☐

        15 seconds pause between sets

Set 2: *Double Iso-Matrix Triad*
        5 full reps
         +
        3 reps one-half up
        3 reps one-half down
         +
        2 reps one-half up (holding in the half position for 3 seconds)
        2 reps one-half down (holding in the half position for 3 seconds)
         +
        5 full reps   ☐

        15 seconds pause between sets

Set 3: *Triple Iso-Matrix Triad*
5 full reps
+
3 reps one-half up
3 reps one-half down
+
3 reps one-half up (holding in the half position for 3 seconds)
3 reps one-half down (holding in the half position for 3 seconds)
+
5 full reps

□

20 seconds pause between sets

Set 4: *Single Mixed Matrix*
5 full reps
+
1 rep one-fifth up
1 rep one-half up
+
1 rep one-fifth down
1 rep one-half down
+
5 full reps

□

Rest 1 minute between exercises

Exercise C: Seated Dumbbell Presses

(Tick the box when you've completed the relevant exercise.)

Set 1: *Single Iso-Matrix Triad*
5 full reps
+
3 reps one-half up
3 reps one-half down
+
1 rep one-half up (holding in the half position for 3 seconds)
1 rep one-half down (holding in the half position for 3 seconds)
+
5 full reps

□

15 seconds pause between sets

Set 2: *Double Iso-Matrix Triad*
    5 full reps
      +
    3 reps one-half up
    3 reps one-half down
      +
    2 reps one-half up (holding in the half position for 3 seconds)
    2 reps one-half down (holding in the half position for 3 seconds)
      +
    5 full reps

    15 seconds pause between sets

Set 3: *Triple Iso-Matrix Triad*
    5 full reps
      +
    3 reps one-half up
    3 reps one-half down
      +
    3 reps one-half up (holding in the half position for 3 seconds)
    3 reps one-half down (holding in the half position for 3 seconds)
      +
    5 full reps

    20 seconds pause between sets

Set 4: *Single Mixed Matrix*
    5 full reps
      +
    1 rep one-fifth up
    1 rep one-half up
      +
    1 rep one-fifth down
    1 rep one-half down
      +
    5 full reps

Rest 3 minutes before proceeding to the next body part exercise

Abdominals

Exercise A: Crunches

(Tick the box when you've completed the relevant exercise.)

Set 1: *Single Iso-Matrix Triad*
　　　 5 full reps
　　　　 +
　　　 3 reps one-half up
　　　 3 reps one-half down
　　　　 +
　　　 1 rep one-half up (holding in the half position for 3 seconds)
　　　 1 rep one-half down (holding in the half position for 3 seconds)
　　　　 +
　　　 5 full reps

　　　 □

　　　 15 seconds pause between sets

Set 2: *Double Iso-Matrix Triad*
　　　 5 full reps
　　　　 +
　　　 3 reps one-half up
　　　 3 reps one-half down
　　　　 +
　　　 2 reps one-half up (holding in the half position for 3 seconds)
　　　 2 reps one-half down (holding in the half position for 3 seconds)
　　　　 +
　　　 5 full reps

　　　 □

　　　 15 seconds pause between sets

Set 3: *Triple Iso-Matrix Triad*
　　　 5 full reps
　　　　 +
　　　 3 reps one-half up
　　　 3 reps one-half down
　　　　 +
　　　 3 reps one-half up (holding in the half position for 3 seconds)
　　　 3 reps one-half down (holding in the half position for 3 seconds)
　　　　 +
　　　 5 full reps

　　　 □

　　　 20 seconds pause between sets

Set 4: *Single Mixed Matrix*
        5 full reps
          +
        1 rep one-fifth up
        1 rep one-half up
          +
        1 rep one-fifth down
        1 rep one-half down
          +
        5 full reps

☐

Rest 1 minute between exercises

Exercise B: Bent-knee Hanging Leg Raises

(Tick the box when you've completed the relevant exercise.)

Set 1: *Single Iso-Matrix Triad*
        5 full reps
          +
        3 reps one-half up
        3 reps one-half down
          +
        1 rep one-half up (holding in the half position for 3 seconds)
        1 rep one-half down (holding in the half position for 3 seconds)
          +
        5 full reps

☐

15 seconds pause between sets

Set 2: *Double Iso-Matrix Triad*
        5 full reps
          +
        3 reps one-half up
        3 reps one-half down
          +
        2 reps one-half up (holding in the half position for 3 seconds)
        2 reps one-half down (holding in the half position for 3 seconds)
          +
        5 full reps

☐

15 seconds pause between sets

Set 3: *Triple Iso-Matrix Triad*
5 full reps
+
3 reps one-half up
3 reps one-half down
+
3 reps one-half up (holding in the half position for 3 seconds)
3 reps one-half down (holding in the half position for 3 seconds)
+
5 full reps

☐

20 seconds pause between sets

Set 4: *Single Mixed Matrix*
5 full reps
+
1 rep one-fifth up
1 rep one-half up
+
1 rep one-fifth down
1 rep one-half down
+
5 full reps

☐

Rest 1 minute between exercises

Exercise C: Rope Pulls

(Tick the box when you've completed the relevant exercise.)

Set 1: *Single Iso-Matrix Triad*
5 full reps
+
3 reps one-half up
3 reps one-half down
+
1 rep one-half up (holding in the half position for 3 seconds)
1 rep one-half down (holding in the half position for 3 seconds)
+
5 full reps

☐

15 seconds pause between sets

Rope Pulls

Set 2: *Double Iso-Matrix Triad*
       5 full reps
          +
       3 reps one-half up
       3 reps one-half down
          +
       2 reps one-half up (holding in the half position for 3 seconds)
       2 reps one-half down (holding in the half position for 3 seconds)
          +
       5 full reps

☐

15 seconds pause between sets

Set 3: *Triple Iso-Matrix Triad*
        5 full reps
            +
        3 reps one-half up
        3 reps one-half down
            +
        3 reps one-half up (holding in the half position for 3 seconds)
        3 reps one-half down (holding in the half position for 3 seconds)
            +
        5 full reps

☐

20 seconds pause between sets

Set 4: *Single Mixed Matrix*
        5 full reps
            +
        1 rep one-fifth up
        1 rep one-half up
            +
        1 rep one-fifth down
        1 rep one-half down
            +
        5 full reps

☐

Finish of Saturday training routine

12 Training routines, months 2 to 12

Month 2 training routine: Matrix sequences for all body parts

Note: The four-set configuration of Matrix principles is rotated each month to include one new Matrix technique as follows.
(Tick the box when you've completed the relevant exercise.)

Set 1: *Double Iso-Matrix Triad*
　　　5 full reps
　　　　+
　　　3 reps half-up
　　　3 reps half-down
　　　　+
　　　2 reps half-up (holding in the half position for 3 seconds)
　　　2 reps half-down (holding in the half position for 3 seconds)
　　　　+
　　　5 full reps

☐

　　　15 seconds pause between sets

Set 2: *Triple Iso-Matrix Triad*
　　　5 full reps
　　　　+
　　　3 reps half-up
　　　3 reps half-down
　　　　+
　　　3 reps half-up (holding in the half position for 3 seconds)
　　　3 reps half-down (holding in the half position for 3 seconds)
　　　　+
　　　5 full reps

☐

　　　15 seconds pause between sets

153

Dumbbell Bench Press

Set 3: *Single Mixed Matrix*
        5 full reps
            +
        1 rep one-fifth up
        1 rep half-up
            +
        1 rep one-fifth down
        1 rep half-down
            +
        5 full reps

        20 seconds pause between sets

Set 4: *Double Mixed Matrix*
        5 full reps
            +
        2 reps one-fifth up
        2 reps half-up
            +
        2 reps one-fifth down
        2 reps half-down
            +
        5 full reps

        Rest 1 minute between exercises
        Rest 3 minutes before proceeding to the next body part

Month 3 training routine: Matrix sequences for all body parts

(Tick the box when you've completed the relevant exercise.)

Set 1: *Triple Iso-Matrix Triad*
     5 full reps
       +
     3 reps half-up
     3 reps half-down
       +
     3 reps half-up (holding in the half position for 3 seconds)
     3 reps half-down (holding in the half position for 3 seconds)
       +
     5 full reps

     □

     15 seconds pause between sets

Set 2: *Single Mixed Matrix*
     5 full reps
       +
     1 rep one-fifth up
     1 rep half-up
       +
     1 rep one-fifth down
     1 rep half-down
       +
     5 full reps

     □

     15 seconds pause between sets

Set 3: *Double Mixed Matrix*
     5 full reps
       +
     2 reps one-fifth up
     2 reps half-up
       +
     2 reps one-fifth down
     2 reps half-down
       +
     5 full reps

     □

     20 seconds pause between sets

Set 4: *Triple Mixed Matrix*
        5 full reps
        +
        3 reps one-fifth up
        3 reps half-up
        +
        3 reps one-fifth down
        3 reps half-up
        +
        5 full reps

☐

Rest 1 minute between exercises
Rest 3 minutes before proceeding to the next body part

Month 4 training routine: Matrix sequences for all body parts

(Tick the box when you've completed the relevant exercise.)

Set 1: *Single Mixed Matrix*
        5 full reps
        +
        1 rep one-fifth up
        1 rep half-up
        +
        1 rep one-fifth down
        1 rep half-down
        +
        5 full reps

☐

15 seconds pause between sets

Set 2: *Double Mixed Matrix*
        5 full reps
        +
        2 reps one-fifth up
        2 reps half-up
        +
        2 reps one-fifth down
        2 reps half-down
        +
        5 full reps

☐

15 seconds pause between sets

Set 3: *Triple Mixed Matrix*
5 full reps
+
3 reps one-fifth up
3 reps half-up
+
3 reps one-fifth down
3 reps half-down
+
5 full reps

☐

20 seconds pause between sets

Set 4: *Single Mixed Iso-Matrix*
5 full reps
+
1 rep one-fifth up (holding for 3 seconds)
1 rep half-up (holding for 3 seconds)
+
1 rep one-fifth down (holding for 3 seconds)
1 rep half-down (holding for 3 seconds)
+
5 full reps

☐

Rest 1 minute between exercises
Rest 3 minutes before proceeding to the next body part

Month 5 training routine: Matrix sequences for all body parts

(Tick the box when you've completed the relevant exercise.)

Set 1: *Double Mixed Matrix*
5 full reps
+
2 reps one-fifth up
2 reps half-up
+
2 reps one-fifth down
2 reps half-down
+
5 full reps

☐

15 seconds pause between sets

Preacher Bench Curls with Dumbbells

Set 2: *Triple Mixed Matrix*
5 full reps
+
3 reps one-fifth up
3 reps half-up
+
3 reps one-fifth down
3 reps half-down
+
5 full reps

□

20 seconds pause between sets

Set 3: *Single Mixed Iso-Matrix*
5 full reps
+
1 rep one-fifth up (holding for 3 seconds)
1 rep half-up (holding for 3 seconds)
+
1 rep one-fifth down (holding for 3 seconds)
1 rep half-down (holding for 3 seconds)
+
5 full reps

□

20 seconds pause between sets

Set 4: *Double Mixed Iso-Matrix*
   5 full reps
      +
   2 reps one-fifth up (holding for 3 seconds)
   2 reps half-up (holding for 3 seconds)
      +
   2 reps one-fifth down (holding for 3 seconds)
   2 reps half-down (holding for 3 seconds)
      +
   5 full reps

☐

   Rest 1 minute between exercises
   Rest 3 minutes before proceeding to the next body part

Month 6 training routine: Matrix sequences for all body parts

(Tick the box when you've completed the relevant exercise.)

Set 1: *Triple Mixed Matrix*
   5 full reps
      +
   3 reps one-fifth up
   3 reps half-up
      +
   3 reps one-fifth down
   3 reps half-up
      +
   5 full reps

☐

   15 seconds pause between sets

Set 2: *Single Mixed Iso-Matrix*
   5 full reps
      +
   1 rep one-fifth up (holding for 3 seconds)
   1 rep half-up (holding for 3 seconds)
      +
   1 rep one-fifth down (holding for 3 seconds)
   1 rep half-down (holding for 3 seconds)
      +
   5 full reps

☐

   20 seconds pause between sets

Set 3: *Double Mixed Iso-Matrix*
    5 full reps
      +
    2 reps one-fifth up (holding for 3 seconds)
    2 reps half-up (holding for 3 seconds)
      +
    2 reps one-fifth down (holding for 3 seconds)
    2 reps half-down (holding for 3 seconds)
      +
    5 full reps

☐

    20 seconds pause between sets

Set 4: *Triple Mixed Iso-Matrix*
    5 full reps
      +
    3 reps one-fifth up (holding for 3 seconds)
    3 reps half-up (holding for 3 seconds)
      +
    3 reps one-fifth down (holding for 3 seconds)
    3 reps half-down (holding for 3 seconds)
      +
    5 full reps

☐

    Rest 1 minute between exercises
    Rest 3 minutes before proceeding to the next body part

Month 7 training routine: Matrix sequences for all body parts

(Tick the box when you've completed the relevant exercise.)

Set 1: *Single Mixed Iso-Matrix*
    5 full reps
      +
    1 rep one-fifth up (holding for 3 seconds)
    1 rep half-up (holding for 3 seconds)
      +
    1 rep one-fifth down (holding for 3 seconds)
    1 rep half-down (holding for 3 seconds)
      +
    5 full reps

☐

    15 seconds pause between sets

Set 2: *Double Mixed Iso-Matrix*
5 full reps
+
2 reps one-fifth up (holding for 3 seconds)
2 reps half-up (holding for 3 seconds)
+
2 reps one-fifth down (holding for 3 seconds)
2 reps half-down (holding for 3 seconds)
+
5 full reps

☐

20 seconds pause between sets

Set 3: *Triple Mixed Iso-Matrix*
5 full reps
+
3 reps one-fifth up (holding for 3 seconds)
3 reps half-up (holding for 3 seconds)
+
3 reps one-fifth down (holding for 3 seconds)
3 reps half-down (holding for 3 seconds)
+
5 full reps

☐

20 seconds pause between sets

Set 4: *Cumulative Iso-Matrix Reversals*
3 full reps
+
3 reps three-quarters up
3 reps three-quarters down
+
4 full reps
+
4 reps three-quarters up
4 reps three-quarters down
+
5 full reps

☐

Rest 1 minute between exercises
Rest 3 minutes before proceeding to the next body part

Month 8 training routine: Matrix sequences for all body parts

(Tick the box when you've completed the relevant exercise.)

Set 1: *Double Mixed Iso-Matrix*
   5 full reps
      +
   2 reps one-fifth up (holding for 3 seconds)
   2 reps half-up (holding for 3 seconds)
      +
   2 reps one-fifth down (holding for 3 seconds)
   2 reps half-down (holding for 3 seconds)
      +
   5 full reps   ☐

   15 seconds pause between sets

Set 2: *Triple Mixed Iso-Matrix*
   5 full reps
      +
   3 reps one-fifth up (holding for 3 seconds)
   3 reps half-up (holding for 3 seconds)
      +
   3 reps one-fifth down (holding for 3 seconds)
   3 reps half-down (holding for 3 seconds)
      +
   5 full reps   ☐

   20 seconds pause between sets

Lateral Raises can be performed with free weights or on a Cable Machine.

Set 3: *Cumulative Iso-Matrix Reversals*
   3 full reps
      +
   3 reps three-quarters up
   3 reps three-quarters down
      +
   4 full reps
      +
   4 reps three-quarters up
   4 reps three-quarters down
      +
   5 full reps

   □

20 seconds pause between sets

Set 4: *Iso-Matrix Alternates*
  5 full reps
    +
  1 rep half-up (holding for 3 seconds)
  1 rep half-down (holding for 3 seconds)
  1 full rep
    +
  1 rep half-up (holding for 3 seconds)
  1 rep half-down (holding for 3 seconds)
  2 full reps
    +
  1 rep half-up (holding for 3 seconds)
  1 rep half-down (holding for 3 seconds)
  3 full reps
    +
  1 rep half-up (holding for 3 seconds)
  1 rep half-down (holding for 3 seconds)
  4 full reps
    +
  1 rep half-up (holding for 3 seconds)
  1 rep half-down (holding for 3 seconds)
  5 full reps

☐

  Rest 1 minute between exercises
  Rest 3 minutes before proceeding to the next body part

Month 9 training routine: Matrix sequences for all body parts

(Tick the box when you've completed the relevant exercise.)

Set 1: *Triple Mixed Iso-Matrix*
  5 full reps
    +
  3 reps one-fifth up (holding for 3 seconds)
  3 reps half-up (holding for 3 seconds)
    +
  3 reps one-fifth down (holding for 3 seconds)
  3 reps half-down (holding for 3 seconds)
    +
  5 full reps

☐

  15 seconds pause between sets

Set 2: *Cumulative Iso-Matrix Reversals*
3 full reps
+
3 reps three-quarters up
3 reps three-quarters down
+
4 full reps
+
4 reps three-quarters up
4 reps three-quarters down
+
5 full reps

☐

20 seconds pause between sets

Set 3: *Iso-Matrix Alternates*
5 full reps
+
1 rep half-up (holding for 3 seconds)
1 rep half-down (holding for 3 seconds)
1 full rep
+
1 rep half-up (holding for 3 seconds)
1 rep half-down (holding for 3 seconds)
2 full reps
+
1 rep half-up (holding for 3 seconds)
1 rep half-down (holding for 3 seconds)
3 full reps
+
1 rep half-up (holding for 3 seconds)
1 rep half-down (holding for 3 seconds)
4 full reps
+
1 rep half-up (holding for 3 seconds)
1 rep half-down (holding for 3 seconds)
5 full reps

☐

20 seconds pause between sets

Set 4: *Mixed Matrix Composites*
5 full reps
+
3 reps one-fifth up
3 reps half-up
+
3 reps one-fifth up
3 reps half-up
+
3 reps one-fifth up
3 reps half-up
+
3 reps one-fifth down
3 reps half-down
+
3 reps one-fifth down
3 reps half-down
+
3 reps one-fifth down
3 reps half-down
+
5 full reps

☐

Rest 1 minute between exercises
Rest 3 minutes before proceeding to the next body part

Month 10 training routine: Matrix sequences for all body parts

(Tick the box when you've completed the relevant exercise.)

Set 1: *Cumulative Iso-Matrix Reversals*
3 full reps
+
3 reps three-quarters up
3 reps three-quarters down
+
4 full reps
+
4 reps three-quarters up
4 reps three-quarters down
+
5 full reps

☐

15 seconds pause between sets

Overhead Press on Smith Machine

Set 2: *Iso-Matrix Alternates*
    5 full reps
      +
    1 rep half-up (holding for 3 seconds)
    1 rep half-down (holding for 3 seconds)
    1 full rep
      +
    1 rep half-up (holding for 3 seconds)
    1 rep half-down (holding for 3 seconds)
    2 full reps
      +
    1 rep half-up (holding for 3 seconds)
    1 rep half-down (holding for 3 seconds)
    3 full reps
      +
    1 rep half-up (holding for 3 seconds)
    1 rep half-down (holding for 3 seconds)
    4 full reps
      +
    1 rep half-up (holding for 3 seconds)
    1 rep half-down (holding for 3 seconds)
    5 full reps

20 seconds pause between sets

Set 3: *Mixed Matrix Composites*
5 full reps
+
3 reps one-fifth up
3 reps half-up
+
3 reps one-fifth up
3 reps half-up
+
3 reps one-fifth up
3 reps half-up
+
3 reps one-fifth down
3 reps half-down
+
3 reps one-fifth down
3 reps half-down
+
3 reps one-fifth down
3 reps half-down
+
5 full reps

20 seconds pause between sets

Set 4: *Single Iso-Matrix Triad*
5 full reps
+
1 rep half-up
1 rep half-down
+
1 rep half-up (holding in the half position for 3 seconds)
1 rep half-down (holding in the half position for 3 seconds)
+
5 full reps

Rest 1 minute between exercises
Rest 3 minutes before proceeding to the next body part

Month 11 training routine: Matrix sequences for all body parts

(Tick the box when you've completed the relevant exercise.)

Set 1: *Iso-Matrix Alternates*

     5 full reps

      +

     1 rep half-up (holding for 3 seconds)

     1 rep half-down (holding for 3 seconds)

     1 full rep

      +

     1 rep half-up (holding for 3 seconds)

     1 rep half-down (holding for 3 seconds)

     2 full reps

      +

     1 rep half-up (holding for 3 seconds)

     1 rep half-down (holding for 3 seconds)

     3 full reps

      +

     1 rep half-up (holding for 3 seconds)

     1 rep half-down (holding for 3 seconds)

     4 full reps

      +

     1 rep half-up (holding for 3 seconds)

     1 rep half-down (holding for 3 seconds)

     5 full reps

     15 seconds pause between sets

Set 2: *Mixed Matrix Composites*
5 full reps
+
3 reps one-fifth up
3 reps half-up
+
3 reps one-fifth up
3 reps half-up
+
3 reps one-fifth up
3 reps half-up
+
3 reps one-fifth down
3 reps half-down
+
3 reps one-fifth down
3 reps half-down
+
3 reps one-fifth down
3 reps half-down
+
5 full reps

20 seconds pause between sets

Set 3: *Single Iso-Matrix Triad*
5 full reps
+
1 rep half-up
1 rep half-down
+
1 rep half-up (holding in the half position for 3 seconds)
1 rep half-down (holding in the half position for 3 seconds)
+
5 full reps

20 seconds pause between sets

Champion bodybuilder, Ian Riley

Set 4: *Double Iso-Matrix Triad*
   5 full reps
      +
   3 reps half-up
   3 reps half-down
      +
   2 reps half-up (holding in the half position for 3 seconds)
   2 reps half-down (holding in the half position for 3 seconds)
      +
   5 full reps

   Rest 1 minute between exercises
   Rest 3 minutes before proceeding to the next body part

Month 12 training routine: Matrix sequences for all body parts

(Tick the box when you've completed the relevant exercise.)

Set 1: *Mixed Matrix Composites*
   5 full reps
      +
   3 reps one-fifth up
   3 reps half-up
      +
   3 reps one-fifth up
   3 reps half-up
      +
   3 reps one-fifth up
   3 reps half-up
      +
   3 reps one-fifth down
   3 reps half-down
      +
   3 reps one-fifth down
   3 reps half-down
      +
   3 reps one-fifth down
   3 reps half-down
      +
   5 full reps

   □

   20 seconds pause between sets

Set 2: *Single Iso-Matrix Triad*
   5 full reps
      +
   1 rep half-up
   1 rep half-down
      +
   1 rep half-up (holding in the half position for 3 seconds)
   1 rep half-down (holding in the half position for 3 seconds)
      +
   5 full reps

   □

   20 seconds pause between sets

Set 3: *Double Iso-Matrix Triad*
    5 full reps
      +
    3 reps half-up
    3 reps half-down
      +
    2 reps half-up (holding in the half position for 3 seconds)
    2 reps half-down (holding in the half position for 3 seconds)
      +
    5 full reps

    20 seconds pause between sets

Set 4: *Triple Iso-Matrix Triad*
    5 full reps
      +
    3 reps half-up
    3 reps half-down
      +
    3 reps half-up (holding in the half position for 3 seconds)
    3 reps half-down (holding in the half position for 3 seconds)
      +
    5 full reps

Rest 1 minute between exercises
Rest 3 minutes before proceeding to the next body part

Appendix: the 36 core Matrix techniques

1   *Conventional Matrix*

5 full reps
+
5 reps half-up
5 reps half-down
+
5 full reps

2   *Descending Matrix*

7 full reps
6 reps half-up
5 reps half-down
4 full reps

3   *Ascending Matrix*

4 full reps
5 reps half-up
6 reps half-down
7 full reps

4   *Matrix Alternates*

5 full reps					
+					
1 rep half-up		1 rep half-up		1 rep half-up	
1 rep half-down	+	1 rep half-down	+	1 rep half-down	
1 full rep		2 full reps		3 full reps	
		1 rep half-up		1 rep half-up	
	+	1 rep half-down	+	1 rep half-down	
		4 full reps		5 full reps	

Leg Extension

5   *Cumulative Matrix Alternates*

1 full rep		2 reps half-up		3 reps half-up		4 reps half-up
1 rep half-up						
1 rep half-down	+	2 reps half-down	+	3 reps half-down	+	4 reps half-down
2 full reps		3 full reps		4 full reps		5 full reps

6   *Matrix Ladders*

5 full reps
\+
1 rep one-fifth up
1 rep two-fifths up   +
1 rep three-fifths up
1 rep four-fifths up
\+
1 full rep

1 rep one-fifth down
1 rep two-fifths down
1 rep three-fifths down
1 rep four-fifths down
1 full rep
\+
5 full reps

7   *Cumulative Matrix Ladders*

1 full rep
\+
1 rep one-fifth up
2 reps two-fifths up   +
3 reps three-fifths up
4 reps four-fifths up
\+
5 full reps

1 rep one-fifth down
2 reps two-fifths down
3 reps three-fifths down
4 reps four-fifths down
\+
5 full reps

8   *Ascending Iso-Matrix*

5 full reps
    +
1 rep half-up (holding weight in the half position for 1 second)
1 rep half-up (holding for 2 seconds)
1 rep half-up (holding for 3 seconds)
1 rep half-up (holding for 4 seconds)
1 rep half-up (holding for 5 seconds)
1 full rep
    +
1 rep half-down (holding weight in the half position for 1 second)
1 rep half-down (holding for 2 seconds)
1 rep half-down (holding for 3 seconds)
1 rep half-down (holding for 4 seconds)
1 rep half-down (holding for 5 seconds)
    +
5 full reps

9   *Descending Iso-Matrix*

5 full reps
    +
1 rep half-up (holding weight in the half position for 5 seconds)
1 rep half-up (holding for 4 seconds)
1 rep half-up (holding for 3 seconds)
1 rep half-up (holding for 2 seconds)
1 rep half-up (holding for 1 second)
    +
1 full rep
    +
1 rep half-down (holding weight in the half position for 5
seconds)
1 rep half-down (holding for 4 seconds)
1 rep half-down (holding for 3 seconds)
1 rep half-down (holding for 2 seconds)
1 rep half-down (holding for 1 second)
    +
5 full reps

10   *Conventional Iso-Matrix*

5 full reps
+
5 reps half-up (holding for 5 seconds)
5 reps half-down (holding for 5 seconds)
+
5 full reps

11   *Cumulative Iso-Matrix*

1 full rep
+
1 rep half-up (holding for 1 second)
2 reps half-up (holding each rep for 2 seconds)
3 reps half-up (holding each rep for 3 seconds)
4 reps half-up (holding each rep for 4 seconds)
+
5 full reps
+
1 rep half-down (holding for 1 second)
2 reps half-down (holding each rep for 2 seconds)
3 reps half-down (holding each rep for 3 seconds)
4 reps half-down (holding each rep for 4 seconds)
+
5 full reps

12   *Mixed Iso-Matrix*

5 full reps
+
3 reps half-up (holding each rep for 3 seconds)
3 reps half-down (no holding)
3 reps half-up (no holding)
3 reps half-down (holding each rep for 3 seconds)
+
5 full reps

13   *Matrix Steps*

5 full reps
+
1 rep half-up
2 reps half-down
3 reps half-up
4 reps half-down
5 reps half-up
6 reps half-down
+
5 full reps

14   *Matrix Giant Steps*

5 full reps
+
1 rep half-up
2 reps half-down
+
3 full reps
+
4 reps half-up
5 reps half-down
+
6 full reps

15   *Iso-Matrix Steps*

1 full rep
+
2 reps half-up (holding each rep for 3 seconds)
3 reps half-down (holding each rep for 3 seconds)
4 reps half-up (holding each rep for 3 seconds)
5 reps half-down (holding each rep for 3 seconds)
+
6 full reps

16   *Cumulative Iso-Matrix Steps*

1 full rep
2 reps half-up (holding each rep for 3 seconds)
3 reps half-down (holding each rep for 4 seconds)
4 reps half-up (holding each rep for 5 seconds)
5 reps half-down (holding each rep for 6 seconds)
+
6 full reps

Seated Dumbbell Curls

17   Iso-Matrix Giant Steps

5 full reps
 +
1 rep half-up (holding for 5 seconds)
2 reps half-down (holding each rep for 4 seconds)
 +
3 full reps
 +
4 reps half-up (holding each rep for 3 seconds)
5 reps half-down (holding each rep for 2 seconds)
 +
6 full reps

18   Matrix Reversals

5 full reps
+
1 rep three-quarters up
1 rep three-quarters down
+
1 rep three-quarters up
1 rep three-quarters down
+
1 rep three-quarters up
1 rep three-quarters down
+
5 full reps

19   Descending Matrix Reversals

7 full reps
+
1 rep three-quarters up
1 rep three-quarters down
+
6 full reps
+
1 rep three-quarters up
1 rep three-quarters down
+
5 full reps

20   Ascending Matrix Reversals

5 full reps
+
1 rep three-quarters up
1 rep three-quarters down
+
6 full reps
+
1 rep three-quarters up
1 rep three-quarters down
+
7 full reps

21   *Cumulative Matrix Reversals*

3 full reps
+
3 reps three-quarters up
3 reps three-quarters down
+
4 full reps
+
4 reps three-quarters up
4 reps three-quarters down
+
5 full reps

22   *Matrix Composites*

5 full reps
+
3 reps half-up
3 reps half-down
+
3 reps half-up
3 reps half-down
+
3 reps half-up
3 reps half-down
+
5 full reps

23   *Matrix Reverse Ladders*

5 full reps
+
1 rep one-fifth up
1 rep one-fifth down
+
1 rep two-fifths up
1 rep two-fifths down
+
1 rep three-fifths up
1 rep three-fifths down
+
1 rep four-fifths up
1 rep four-fifths down
+
5 full reps

24   *Matrix Reverse Step Ladders*

1 full rep
   +
2 reps one-fifth up
3 reps one-fifth down
   +
4 reps two-fifths up
5 reps two-fifths down
   +
6 reps three-fifths up
7 reps three-fifths down
   +
8 reps four-fifths up
9 reps four-fifths down
   +
10 full reps

25   *Single Iso-Matrix Triad*

5 full reps
   +
3 reps half-up
3 reps half-down
   +
1 rep half-up (holding in the half-up position for 3 seconds)
1 rep half-down (holding in the half-down position for 3 seconds)
   +
5 full reps

26   *Double Iso-Matrix Triad*

5 full reps
   +
3 reps half-up
3 reps half-down
   +
2 reps half-up (holding in the half-up position for 3 seconds)
2 reps half-down (holding in the half-down position for 3
seconds)
   +
5 full reps

27   *Triple Iso-Matrix Triad*

5 full reps
+
3 reps half-up
3 reps half-down
3 reps half-up (holding in the half-up position for 3 seconds)
3 reps half-down (holding in the half-down position for 3 seconds)
+
5 full reps

28   *Single Mixed Matrix*

5 full reps
+
1 rep one-fifth up
1 rep half-up
+
1 rep one-fifth down
1 rep half-down
+
5 full reps

29   *Double Mixed Matrix*

5 full reps
+
2 reps one-fifth up
2 reps half-up
+
2 reps one-fifth down
2 reps half-down
5 full reps

30   *Triple Mixed Matrix*

5 full reps
+
3 reps one-fifth up
3 reps half-up
+
3 reps one-fifth down
3 reps half-down
+
5 full reps

31   Single Mixed Iso-Matrix

5 full reps
+
1 rep one-fifth up (holding for 3 seconds)
1 rep half-up (holding for 3 seconds)
+
1 rep one-fifth down (holding for 3 seconds)
1 rep half-down (holding for 3 seconds)
+
5 full reps

32   Double Mixed Iso-Matrix

5 full reps
+
2 reps one-fifth up (holding for 3 seconds)
2 reps half-up (holding for 3 seconds)
+
2 reps one-fifth down (holding for 3 seconds)
2 reps half-down (holding for 3 seconds)
+
5 full reps

33   Triple Mixed Iso-Matrix

5 full reps
+
3 reps one-fifth up (holding for 3 seconds)
3 reps half-up (holding for 3 seconds)
+
3 reps one-fifth down (holding for 3 seconds)
3 reps half-down (holding for 3 seconds)
+
5 full reps

34   *Cumulative Iso-Matrix Reversals*

3 full reps
   +
3 reps three-quarters up
3 reps three-quarters down
   +
4 full reps
   +
4 reps three-quarters up
4 reps three-quarters down
   +
5 full reps

35   *Iso-Matrix Alternates*

5 full reps
   +
1 rep half-up (holding for 3 seconds)
1 rep half-down (holding for 3 seconds)
1 full rep
   +
1 rep half-up (holding for 3 seconds)
1 rep half-down (holding for 3 seconds)
2 full reps
   +
1 rep half-up (holding for 3 seconds)
1 rep half-down (holding for 3 seconds)
3 full reps
   +
1 rep half-up (holding for 3 seconds)
1 rep half-down (holding for 3 seconds)
4 full reps
   +
1 rep half-up (holding for 3 seconds)
1 rep half-down (holding for 3 seconds)
5 full reps

36   *Mixed Matrix Composites*

5 full reps
+
3 reps one-fifth up
3 reps half-up
+
3 reps one-fifth up
3 reps half-up
+
3 reps one-fifth up
3 reps half-up
+
3 reps one-fifth down
3 reps half-down
+
3 reps one-fifth down
3 reps half-down
+
3 reps one-fifth down
3 reps half-down
+
5 full reps

Notes

2 Weights and repetitions

1 John Little, 'Muscle-fiber recruitment', in *Flex* (USA), September 1993, p. 176.
2 Douglas M. Crist, 'All circuits go', in *Muscle & Fitness* (USA), April 1993, p. 100.
3 John Little, op. cit., p. 176.
4 Douglas M. Crist, op. cit., p. 186.
5 ibid., p. 100.
6 On types of muscle fibre, see R. S. Laura and K. R. Dutton, *Matrix for Muscle Gain*, Sydney: Allen & Unwin, 1993, p. 10.
7 John Little, 'Power factor training', in *Flex* (USA), September 1993, p. 102.
8 Crist, op. cit., p. 186.
9 John Little, op. cit.
10 Reported on *Quantum*, ABC TV (Australia), 16 February 1994.
11 See the discussion on the biomechanics of sprinting in R. S. Laura and K. R. Dutton, *Weight Training for Sports*, Sydney: Bantam, 1993, pp. 15–16.
12 Paul Ward, 'Can computers build muscle?', in *Muscle & Fitness* (USA), August 1993, p. 245.

3 Isolation and awareness

1 Michael Yessis, 'Isolating smaller muscles', in *Muscle & Fitness* (USA), June 1993, p. 38.
2 Daniel McCarthy with Nancy McCarthy, 'Psyching: is your method halting muscle growth?', in *Muscle & Fitness* (Australia), December 1993, pp. 50–1.
3 John Tristany, 'Psychophysiology', in *Flex* (USA), July 1993, pp. 149 ff.
4 See Maxwell Maltz, *Psycho-Cybernetics*, New York: Pocket Books, 1975 (first published 1960), p. 35.
5 Michael Hutchinson, 'Mind over matter = muscle', in *Muscle & Fitness* (USA), July 1993, p. 228.
6 See Marvin Karlins and Lewis B. Andrews, *Biofeedback: Turning on the Power of Your Mind*, Philadelphia/New York: J. B. Lippincott, 1972, p. 26.

7   American Association of Engineering Committee; see *Electrical Engineering*, 70 (October 1951), p. 105.
8   Hugh Downs, in Foreword to Barbara Brown, *New Mind, New Body*, New York: Harper & Row, 1974, p. 105.
9   Brown, op. cit., p. 4.
10 Steven Locke and Douglas Colligan, *The Healer Within: The New Medicine of Mind and Body*, New York: E. P. Dutton, 1986, p. 14.
11 Karlins and Andrews, op. cit., p. 27.
12 See Douglas Carroll, *Biofeedback in Practice*, London: Longman, 1984, p. 116; cf. Malcolm Lader, 'Psychophysiological research and psychosomatic medicine', in *Physiology, Emotion and Psychosomatic Illness*, Amsterdam: Elsevier, 1972, p. 308.
13 See James C. Houk and W. Zev Rymer, 'Neural control of muscle length and tension', in *Handbook of Physiology, Section I: The Nervous System*, Vol. II, Motor Control, Part 1, Bethesda, Maryland: American Physiological Society, 1981, p. 260.
14 See Peter M. H. Rack, 'Limitations of somatosensory feedback in control of posture and movement', in *Handbook of Physiology*, I, II, 1, p. 229.
15 ibid., p. 230.
16 Houk and Rymer, op. cit., pp. 257–8.
17 ibid., p. 312.
18 D. I. McCloskey, 'Corollary discharges: motor commands and perception', in *Handbook of Physiology*, I, II, 1, pp. 1415–47.
19 ibid., pp. 1422–23.
20 ibid., pp. 1424–25.
21 ibid., pp. 1426–28.
22 ibid., p. 1428.
23 See Lyall Watson, *Beyond Supernature*, London: Hodder & Stoughton, 1986, pp. 76–7.
24 See S. C. Gandevia et al., 'Respiratory sensations, cardiovascular control, kinaesthesia and transcranial stimulation during paralysis in humans', in *The Journal of Physiology*, Vol. 470, October 1993, p. 86.
25 Maltz, op. cit., pp. 31–2.
26 ibid., p. 35.
27 See J. V. Basmajian, 'Conscious control and training of motor units and motor neurons', *Muscles Alive: Their Functions Revealed by Electromyography*, Baltimore: Williams & Wilkins, 4th edn., 1979, pp. 115 ff.
28 Barbara Brown, op. cit., p. 173.
29 ibid., p. 169.
30 See R. S. Laura and K. R. Dutton, *Matrix for Muscle Gain*, Sydney: Allen & Unwin, 1993, p. 9.
31 Brown, op. cit., p. 170.

4 Health and the mind

1   R. S. Laura, in Ronald S. Laura and Saxon W. White, *Drug Controversy in Sport: The Socio-Ethical and Medical Issues*, Sydney: Allen & Unwin, 1991, p. 12.

2 Dr Larry Dossey, *Healing Breakthroughs: How Your Attitudes and Beliefs Can Affect Your Health*, London: Platkus, 1991, p. 109.

3 See Steven Locke and Douglas Colligan, *The Healer Within: The New Medicine of Mind and Body*, New York: E. P. Dutton, 1986, pp. 20–1.

4 R. Ader, D. L. Felten and N. Cohen (eds), *Psychoneuroimmunology*, 2nd edn, New York: Academic Press (Harcourt Brace Jovanovich), 1991.

5 *Newcastle Herald* (Australia), 25 February 1994, *The Sydney Morning Herald*, 23 April 1994.

6 John Dwyer, *The Body at War: The Story of Our Immune System*, reported in *The Sydney Morning Herald*, 19 February 1994.

7 See Locke and Colligan, op. cit., pp 130–2.

8 Harvey B. Simon, 'Exercise and Human Immune Function', in R. Ader, D. E. Felten and N. Cohen (eds), op. cit., p. 873.

9 ibid., p. 879.

10 J. G. Cannon and M. J. Kluger, 'Endogenous pyrogen activity in human plasma after exercise', in *Science*, 220 (1983), pp. 617–18.

11 Simon, op. cit., pp. 880–1, 890.

12 ibid., p. 890.

13 Bob Lefavi, PhD, CSCS, and Tom Deters, DC, 'Exercise . . .', in *Muscle & Fitness* (USA), March 1993, p. 176; references p. 242.

14 Locke and Colligan, op. cit., pp. 178–9.

15 *Los Angeles Times* report, quoted in *The Sydney Morning Herald*, 6 November 1993 and 27 November 1993.

16 David L. Felten, 'A personal perspective on psychoneuroimmunology', in Ader, Felten and Cohen (eds), op. cit., p. 1117.

17 Reported in *The Sydney Morning Herald*, 21 March 1994.

18 'Alternative Medicine', in *Choice* magazine (Australia), October 1993, p. 9.

19 'Mind over matter = muscle', in *Muscle & Fitness* (USA), July 1993, pp. 152. ff.

Acknowledgments

The authors gratefully acknowledge the assistance of the following people without whom this final volume in the Matrix trilogy could not have been brought to publication. There is first of all our typist, Ms Shelagh Lummis, who produced the final manuscript in record time and with admirable accuracy. We also express our gratitude to our main photographer, John Freund, whose training photos illustrate most of the exercises included in *The Ultimate Matrix System*. Our thanks also to David Adermann for the studio shots of Adam Laura and to John Terilli for the photos of his outstanding physique. Last, but not least, the authors would like to express their appreciation to the trainers who modelled for the photos: Mose Alatise, Aaron Bennett, Tim Eggert, Paul Harris, Robert Joncevski, Trevor Lasky, Sharon Laura, Adam Laura, Jason Low, Richard Marshall, Corrine McMillan, Deborah Moore, Adam Parer, Scott Parrey, Rahul Prasad, Ian Riley, Drew Swan, Brian Swetnam, John Terilli and Anthony Wingett.

Other books by Ronald S. Laura and Kenneth R. Dutton

The Matrix Principle
Ronald S. Laura and Kenneth R. Dutton

Matrix for Muscle Gain
Ronald S. Laura and Kenneth R. Dutton

Twelve Weeks to a Better Body for Women
Ronald S. Laura and Kenneth R. Dutton

Twelve Weeks to a Better Body for Men
Ronald S. Laura and Kenneth R. Dutton

The Perfectible Body
The Western ideal of physical development
Kenneth R. Dutton

THE MATRIX PRINCIPLE

By Ronald S. Laura and Kenneth R. Dutton

The Matrix Principle introduces the MATRIX System, a major breakthrough in weight training for all those seeking to build a healthy and muscular physique **without the use of harmful drugs**.

Using clear and comprehensive instructions, *The Matrix Principle* provides a complete set of workout routines for each body part. It introduces trainers to the most effective methods of aerobic, isometric and isotonic weight training as well as the most recent advances in exercise physiology, explaining how and why muscles grow and why some forms of exercise are more effective than others in fostering muscle development.

The Matrix Principle is for all trainers at all levels from amateur and professional sports people and contest winning bodybuilders to those just wanting to improve their general fitness.

MATRIX FOR MUSCLE GAIN

By Ronald S. Laura and Kenneth R. Dutton

Following the runaway success of *The Matrix Principle* which established Ron Laura and Ken Dutton's revolutionary concept as a major force in international weight training and bodybuilding, comes *Matrix for Muscle Gain*. Written for those people who have at least a year's weight training experience, the techniques and the programme in this book are directed at increasing muscle mass and muscle definition **without the use of steroids or other drugs**.

Designed to take advantage of the most recent findings in exercise science, *Matrix for Muscle Gain* offers a theoretical base to MATRIX training by explaining the physiology of muscle growth. It also provides general nutritional and diet advice specific to the programme.

By the end of the *Matrix for Muscle Gain* programme, weight trainers should be well equipped for competitive bodybuilding. Those trainers not interested in competing will have achieved an impressive degree of muscularity.

TWELVE WEEKS TO A BETTER BODY FOR WOMEN
TWELVE WEEKS TO A BETTER BODY FOR MEN

By Ronald S. Laura and Kenneth R. Dutton

These two compact books show how a revolutionary form of light-weight exercise can be used to tone up the most out-of-shape body.

The revolutionary MATRIX System, which has proved itself several times more effective than conventional exercise methods, has now been adapted to meet the needs of men and women who have never exercised before or who have let themselves get out of condition. The daily exercise programmes require no special equipment and are easy to follow and simple to perform. Helpful dietary advice is also provided.